CHICAGO PUBLIC LIBRARY

R01082 81910

D1290568

Keep the Memories

Bury the Love

MUSIC INFORMATION CENTER
VISUAL & PERFORMING ARTS
CHICAGO PUBLIC LIBRARY

Keep the Memories
Bury the Love

Karen Tritt Ryon

Eggman Publishing, Inc.

© 1995 Eggman Publishing, Inc. All rights reserved.

Written permission must be received from the publisher before using or reproducing any portion of this book, other than for the purpose of critical reviews or articles.

For interviews and other information call:
1-800-396-4676

ISBN: 1-886371-19-9

Eggman Publishing, Inc.
2909 Poston Avenue, Suite 203
Nashville, TN 37203
(615) 327-9390

R01082 81910

MUSIC INFORMATION CENTER
VISUAL & PERFORMING ARTS
CHICAGO PUBLIC LIBRARY

THE
CHICAGO PUBLIC
LIBRARY

DEDICATION

For my beloved Casey...being your mother is my greatest joy.

SPECIAL THANKS

To the staff of Eggman Publishing, for all their hard work.

To Donna and Burge, who continue to teach me the Art of Being Successful. I love you both. Thank you for being with me before, during, and after.

To Becki J. and Julia A., my girlfriends extraordinaire! Thank you for encouraging me to believe in myself when there was little hope.

To Barbara Lassiter, who was there for me when I needed help.

To Sue, Josh, and Nikki, for enriching my life. I love you and I'll always be eternally grateful to have you as family.

To my mother, Jacque Binette. Words will never express how much I love you. Thank you for supporting me in all my wishes and dreams.

A very special Thank-You to Travis...for showing me how wonderful true love can feel.

April 1985

Dear Karen,

"I am writing this letter to let you know that as far as I'm concerned... it's over. I don't know who you are anymore. You are certainly not the girl I married. Somewhere along the way, you changed. I don't like who you've become. I love you more than anything I've ever known and I guess I always will. But obviously, our love for each other is not enough to keep us going. Even though I know in my heart that this is it, I will always keep the door open just a bit... just in case. As for now... keep the memories, but bury the love." Travis

It is 7:51 pm on a crisp, cool night: Marietta, Georgia, October 1992. I sit curled up on my sofa with a bowl of popcorn on my lap, a warm, fuzzy cat named Labrynth at my feet, and a funny thumping in my heart. In nine very short minutes, my ex-husband, the first true love of my life, will be co-hosting the Academy of Country Music awards in front of millions of people. Why do I feel all this nervous anxiety for him? Maybe it's because I, more than anyone else, know how nervous he really is. He and I were together throughout the very early days of his career, and we both know his true character, but the vast majority of his fans do not. That's all about to change. As the introductory music for the awards show begins, I hurry upstairs to quickly kiss my son goodnight and thank my lucky stars that I am no longer Mrs. Travis Tritt. I am not cut out for the life that Travis has made for himself; frankly, I'm not sure that Travis is either. As I snuggle down on the sofa to watch the show, Clint Black, a real "gentleman's gentleman", is about to announce the "fastest-rising young man in country music today." As I watch Travis, I begin to remember the early years of our relationship. It's not often that I allow myself to think of that time in my life, because I was hurt so deeply. Who among us would, if given the choice, choose to relive the pain of a third-degree burn, or the anguish of seeing a beloved pet put to sleep, or the humiliation we felt the first time we realized that we had really let our parents down? My life with Travis felt like all these things and more—much more. Some memories are too painful to relive, and even the good memories can be unbearable to recall. As I begin, after ten long years, to delve into the past, one question continually comes to mind... Who would have ever thought?

Chapter One

I had just come in from school when the phone rang. A somewhat popular junior in high school, I had a large circle of friends. I was sure that it was one of them calling to tell me the latest gossip. Was I ever wrong! I grabbed the phone. "Hello?"

"Is Karen there?" asked a strange voice. "This is she," I replied.

"I don't think that you know me, but my name is Travis Tritt."

"Know you?" I thought. "Everybody in the whole school knows you! There aren't that many guys who play a guitar, wear cowboy clothes, including boots and a big western hat to school every day. You are the biggest nerd in school, and I can't figure out why you would be calling me!" What I actually said was "Yes, I think I know who you are—what can I do for you?"

"Well, even though you've never really met me, I think you are very pretty, and I was wondering if you would like to go out this Friday night."

I looked at my mother, who was standing in the kitchen trying to decide what to make for dinner. I started waving my arms to get her attention. When she finally looked my way, I started making a goofy face and pointing to the phone. She just laughed and shook her head. "Well, Travis," I said, "I'm actually dating someone right now. Haven't you noticed the class ring that I'm wearing?"

"No, I hadn't noticed. Well, I'm sorry I bothered you. Maybe we could do it some other time," he said. I hung up the phone thinking "Not in a million years!" My mom looked at me quizzically and asked "Who was that?"

"Only the weirdest guy in the whole school," I replied. "His name is Travis Tritt. Can you believe his mother actually named him that? He's this drugstore cowboy at school. He wears western clothes and a big straw cowboy hat with feathers hanging down the back every day! While the other guys are playing football and baseball, he sits in the bleachers playing country music on his guitar. I remember in the sixth grade, a bunch of us kids were playing battle ball in the gym, and there sat Travis, all by himself in the stands, playing his guitar. He's really weird, Mom. No girl in her right mind would be caught dead with him. I can't believe he actually called to ask me out! God, I hope nobody finds out about this. I would never be able to hold my head up in school again."

"Is he all that bad?" my mother asked.

"Worse," I groaned. If anyone had told me at that moment that only one year later I would fall hopelessly in love with Travis Tritt, I would have told them that they were out of their mind.

December 1980

I was a sophisticated, know-it-all senior. I was like every other seventeen-year-old girl on the planet—no one could tell me a thing because I knew it all. My girlfriend Tara and I were going to a concert to benefit the less fortunate children of Atlanta, and in addition to the admission ticket, we were asked to bring a toy for a needy child. Clutching a white stuffed teddy bear, I made my way through the crowd and the biting wind into the welcome heat of the Omni, a huge concert hall that hosted events like the Ringling Brothers' Barnum and Bailey Circus, Atlanta Hawks basketball games, and last but certainly not least, the all-important annual Monster Truck and

Tractor Pull. That night, everyone had turned out to see Hall and Oates, Linda Ronstadt and Andy Gibb. The Omni seats well over fifteen thousand people, and it would seem almost impossible to see someone you know there. As I look back on it now, I think that God must have had a master plan in mind, because Tara and I were seated only five or six rows up from Travis and a bunch of his cowboy friends. There was a no-alcohol rule at the Omni, generally ignored by concert-goers. Teenagers usually brought in whatever they could convince some older guy at the liquor store to buy for them. Tara and I had decided to forgo the liquor. But, lo and behold, there sat Travis with a bottle of Jack Daniels and a container of whiskey sour mix, acting for all the world like the local bartender. Tara grabbed my arm and said "Look down there! It's the guy from school with the guitar. Come on, let's go say hello."

"No, I don't think so," I said. I had not spoken to Travis since that day in September when he called to ask me out. I felt a little awkward, and didn't want to put myself in a position where he would actually think I was interested in him. But Tara insisted, and I eventually agreed to her plan. We quickly jumped down to where the guys were sitting. Tara, never one to be shy, immediately asked if she could have a drink. "Sure," Travis said. He made one and gave it to her, then turned to me and said, "Would you like one, Karen?"

"Well, okay. Just a little one. I don't drink that much," I replied. He poured me a drink. I took it and sat in my seat as far away from him as possible. He kept staring at me, and it was making me very uncomfortable.

Just a few weeks earlier, my parents had taken my brothers and me to see a "Friday the 13th" movie. Travis and a friend of his were sitting in the row directly behind us, shouting warnings at the unsuspecting camp counselors on the screen. They were yelling things like "Watch out, Hoss!" and "Hey man, you'd better get that little filly out of there!" The more they shouted, the further down in my seat I scooted. My mother said that they were trying to impress me—I was sure that they were trying to humiliate me. At one point, Travis said "If I was there, I would blow him away with my Smith and Wesson." "How nice," I thought. "Now, I know he is a hat-wearing, guitar-playing GUN-TOTING redneck!"

I had resolved then that I would never get within ten feet of him; now, here I was sitting next to him at the Omni. The concert continued, and we didn't pay too much attention to each other. Hall and Oates had started to play "If You Leave Me Now." What happened next has never ceased to amaze me. Travis stood up, took my hand, and pulled me to my feet. The hall had darkened to set the mood for the soft romantic ballad. As he put his arms around me and started gently swaying to the music, I felt the first tidal wave of emotion sweep me off my feet. I had never felt like that in my life, and all he had done was touch me. He pulled away and looked at me with those blue eyes. His face was only about four inches from mine, and I could tell from his stunned look that he had felt it too. I was mesmerized. He leaned forward slowly and kissed me very, very softly. To this day, I only have to close my eyes to remember what that kiss felt like. I wish I could recall a phrase from one of the romance novels that could accurately describe that kiss. I can only say that I literally felt I was falling, as if I had been pushed me from an airplane at thirty thousand feet, and I was elated to go. That kiss lasted a lifetime. When it was over, our lips parted, he leaned his forehead against mine, and we stood that way for several minutes... eyes closed, bodies shaking, trying so hard just to catch our breath. I stood there thinking, "Oh, my God! I just fell in love with him. How can this be? My life will never be the same again." I was right. That song was the last of the evening. As the house lights came up, I grabbed my purse, grabbed my friend, and ran. I guess that Travis sensed my turmoil, because he let me go without another word spoken. I was very quiet during the ride home, but Tara could not resist teasing me about kissing the "school cowboy". I didn't care. It was the most incredible night of my life, and I really didn't care if my best friend understood or not. I never believed in love at first sight, but I knew that I loved that boy with all my heart and soul. When Tara dropped me off at my house, I went in and started back toward my bedroom where I could contemplate what had happened. I must have looked a little dazed, because my dad asked "Are you okay? How was the concert?" "I'm wonderful," I replied dreamily, "Concert was great. I'm going to bed now."

I'm sure they thought that I was intoxicated, and in truth, new love feels exactly like that. I slept fitfully, and woke up with a smile on my face and a little bit of panic on my mind. What if I had misinterpreted his reaction? What if he didn't feel the same way I did? What if he never spoke to me again? What was I going to say to him the next time I saw him? All of these thoughts were needless, because an hour later he called. "Hi," he said in his soft Southern drawl. "Hey," I replied just as softly. I was flattered that he had kept my phone number after I had turned him down for a date fifteen months earlier. "Give me directions to your house," he said. "I'm coming over. I have to see you again. I can't stop thinking about you." Without hesitation, I gave him directions. I hung up the phone and ran to take a shower. My parents and brothers were gone for the day, so I had the house all to myself. I sat on the sofa wearing old blue jeans and one of my dad's old button-down shirts, considerably less well-dressed than I had been the night before. I was looking out the window waiting for him to arrive. I realized that I didn't even know what kind of car he drove.

You have to remember that to a seventeen-year-old girl, a boy's car is definitely a status symbol. It's better, for instance, if your boyfriend drives a sports car than if he drives a pick-up truck. When Travis pulled into my driveway in a bright blue, beat-up 1969 Rambler with the primer showing through, all I could think was "He's here! I don't care if he's riding a mule—he's here!" When he walked in the door, I felt my breath catch in my throat and my heart skip a beat. How could one person affect me so dramatically? We stood in my living room for what seemed an eternity, just staring at each other.

5

Then he walked over to me, wrapped his arms around me, and held me for the longest time. I had never felt so utterly complete. It felt so right to be in his arms. I felt warm all over and there was a funny feeling in my stomach. I wasn't experienced enough with men to know that a large part of what I was feeling was pure desire. It was as if the lower part of my body had turned into melting butter. My legs started shaking, and I knew that I had better sit down before I fell down. We sat on the sofa and started talking. There was none of the shyness of the previous night, just open honest communication between two people who knew they had finally found each other. We talked about our surprise at the intensity of our emotions, and how we were both utterly amazed at the way in which they had exploded. Looking into my eyes, he said, "I have never felt this way about anyone. I know, deep in the bottom of my heart, that I am going to spend the rest of my life with you." I just nodded my head in agreement as I stared at him in wonder. I couldn't take my eyes off him. I searched his face, looking for answers to unspoken questions: "Where've you been? How can we possibly feel this way? How have I been living and breathing without you?" The feelings were so overwhelming and yet so frightening. Just being in the same room with him made me feel pretty and sexy and whole. I truly felt as if I had been but half a person and now I was complete. I never wanted to be out of his presence again. He could only stay for a little while, but before he left, we made a date for December 27th. He said he would pick me up at 7:30. Because it was the Christmas holiday, we both had to attend several family engagements, so the 27th was the first free night that we both had. As he left, I was a little distressed not to be on the receiving end of one of his kisses! As he reached the door, he turned around, bumped into me (which was unavoidable, since I was only about two inches behind him), laughed, and kissed me very passionately. If I'd had any doubts about the feelings I had experienced the night before, his kiss completely erased them. How did he learn to do that? I had never seen him with a girl, yet he kissed as though he had been doing it since kindergarten! We said goodbye and he promised to call me that night, leaving me to wonder how I was going to survive until our date.

Chapter Two

Survive I did, and the eagerly-awaited night arrived. I didn't have any of the usual first-date dilemmas about what to wear, how to fix my hair, what perfume to wear, or anything else. From day one, it was as though we'd been together for a hundred years, and I knew that outward appearances weren't important. What mattered most was how we felt, so I put on my most comfortable jeans and a green velour top that I had received as a Christmas gift. The only thing I was nervous about was how my parents would react to him. Before Travis, I had been dating what my parents called "The Good Ones"—school jocks with nice cars, nice looks, and nice families. I feared what they would think of Travis, but I knew that their opinions wouldn't sway my feelings for him in the slightest. We heard him drive up long before we actually saw the car. My dad said, "What is making all that horrible racket?" The words were hardly out of his mouth before the "racket" pulled into the driveway. "He's here!" I sang out as I ran to the door. I flung it open and stood there with a huge grin. Travis and his good friend Jay from the concert were standing on my front porch in full cowboy regalia. I can't remember what Jay was wearing, but to this day I can remember exactly what Travis had on. I should—my mother has never let me forget it nor live it down. Travis wore tight jeans, a black cowboy shirt with white snap buttons and large red roses embroidered on its upper half, an enormous black felt Stetson hat, and a turkey-feather hat band with feathers trailing down his back. I thought he was gorgeous! My parents, on the other hand, were not as impressed. I grabbed his hand and pulled him into the house. Jay followed. "Mom, Dad, this is Travis Tritt." My father shook his hand and my mother, noticing the glazed look in my eyes, put two and two together and pushed me into the kitchen. "Oh, no!" she said in horror. "Not this one! Please tell me that this isn't the one!" I just smiled and nodded my head. Mom groaned audibly and leaned against the refrigerator for support.

"What about Blake?" she asked. "He's a nice young man. He goes to college, he plays baseball, and he seems so nice. Besides, we know his parents and we really like them. We thought you two were an item. What happened?"

"He's not Travis," I replied. I could tell that they didn't approve, but it didn't matter to me. I was in love in the way that only a seventeen-year-old can be. I hugged Mom and told her not to worry; I knew that everything would work out perfectly. We left the house and rode to pick up Jay's date in the Rambler. As soon as we were in the car, Jay turned to Travis and said, "Boy, her Mama hated me! She didn't like you, but she HATED me!" The remainder of the ride is vague, but I do remember that my bottom hurt because the springs in the seat were sticking up through the upholstery. I didn't care—my dream man owned this car. After picking up Jay's date, we drove up to Acworth, Georgia, to the house of a friend of Travis'. Jerry was four or five years older than we were and a builder. He had built a nice little three-bedroom cabin-style house for himself, complete with a front porch and a set of rocking chairs. Jerry's house was the main hangout for Travis and his friends. I met other people there that I had seen around school. Tinsley and Tim, two brothers who were funny and very nice, Jerry and his date Christine, and a few others. We all talked for a while, drinking beer and clowning around. Then, as if on some invisible cue, everyone paired off and went into a

10

separate room of the house. All of the people without dates left, and only the couples remained. Travis and I found ourselves on the living room floor in front of a cozy fire. We lay in each others' arms for a while. He was kissing me and whispering words of love and passion in my ear. I felt delirious with pleasure, every nerve ending in my body alive and tingling. Travis pulled me up so that I was sitting on his lap, facing him. He put his hands in my hair, pulled me to him, and lightly kissed me and nibbled at my lower lip. He pulled back and gently traced my face with his fingertips. Travis softly said, "Open your eyes," then he quietly slipped his class ring off his finger and laid it in the palm of my hand. "I love you and I want you to always wear it. Will you promise me that?" Even though I had worn a boy's class ring before, I felt so honored to wear this particular one. I slipped it on my finger, mentally wondering how much tape I was going to have to wrap around it in order to make it fit. I looked down at the pretty amber stone that flickered in the firelight and the words circling it: "Sprayberry High School Class of 1981".

"I promise," I said. Even though we weren't officially married until the fall of 1982, that was the moment that I wed Travis in my heart. I took this commitment very seriously. No one had ever made me feel as wonderful as he did. I wanted to cry from the sheer joy of loving him and knowing that he loved me. Then, he bent down and gave me another one of those wonderful kisses. We kissed, or "made out" as we called it in those days, for hours, literally hours. Only teenagers can kiss that long or that intently. If I had had any doubts about my love for him, they were all erased that night. I loved him, but I wasn't about to tell him that. Something about the timing wasn't right. I was immature enough to want him to wonder about my feelings for him. The next day, he asked me why I hadn't told him that I loved him in return. I answered coyly, "Do you want me to say it now just because you did? Wouldn't you rather wait and have me say it when I really mean it?"

He was visibly taken aback and said, "Well, I guess I'd rather know that you really felt that way before you said it." So I left him dangling on a string... for three whole days, until New Year's Eve, 1981. Travis had invited me over to his house to celebrate. He lived in a middle-class house in a middle-class subdivision. This would also be the first time that I met his mother. He had explained to me that his parents had recently divorced, and that she had bought the house with her part of the settlement. She lived there with Travis and his twelve-year-old sister Sheilah. When I entered the house, his mother Gwen greeted me warmly. Sheilah just stared for a while. It was obvious to me that very few girls had been brought home by Travis to meet "Mama". I don't know this for a fact, but I daresay that I was the first. His Mom let us order a pizza and gave us a bottle of non-alcoholic champagne to drink at midnight. I couldn't have known it at that time, but this would become a tradition in our relationship—pizza and champagne every New Year's Eve. Then Gwen and Sheilah left us alone. Travis took me on a tour of the house, and imagine my surprise when I went into his room and found a normal teenage boy's room with one large exception. Covering one entire wall was a painting of the ocean with a huge cartoon whale in the middle. I put my hand over my mouth to stifle a laugh; he looked at me sheepishly and said, "That was here when we moved in. Obviously, this was a little boy's room."

"Obviously," I replied. In the days to come I would yearn to tell my friends about the big blue whale in Travis' room, but I didn't want him to be teased about it. We went downstairs, ate our pizza, cleaned up, and sat down on the sofa to snuggle and await the arrival of the New Year. It was an ordinary sofa, covered with crushed velour in a geometric pattern of earth tones, primarily rust and brown. I had no clue that this old velour couch would become a focal point in our divorce in June 1984. Travis left me for a moment to go upstairs. When he returned, he was carrying a beat-up guitar case. He opened it and pulled out a beautiful Epiphone twelve-string guitar. I curled up on the sofa, and we played a scene that was to be repeated hundreds of times in our three-and-a-half-year relationship—Travis playing his guitar and singing to me while I sat with an enraptured look on my face. The very first song that Travis ever sang to me was "Lady" by John Denver. I have to admit that it made me cry then and still does to this day. It's a beautiful song on its own, but even more moving when it's being sung to you by someone who had a voice like Travis'. He went on to sing "Annie's Song" and "Follow Me," also by John Denver. He and I both were big John Denver fans. I had no idea that he was a songwriter until he sang a song called "Spend a Little Time" that he had written when he was only fourteen years old. It's a sad ballad about a lonely boy pleading with a girl to just spend a little time with him. (If she did, she would realize how much he loves her.) I've often wondered why he never recorded that song. As I sat there listening to him, I considered the irony of the situation. For years in school, I had avoided Travis and his band like the black plague. We had school functions every year like the "Spring Fling" and the "Winter Wingding," events that the school held to celebrate the arrival of a season. We usually had shorter classes and sack lunches that could be eaten outside, picnic style. Like clockwork, Travis always played country music with his little band. I steered clear of him during the events, but here I was a captive audience of one, loving every minute of it. I must admit that I disliked country music at first, but I grew to love it and still listen to it today. I can't remember if he grew tired of playing or if I grew tired of listening... more than likely the latter, I think. He put the guitar away and poured us a glass of "champagne" in little plastic champagne glasses his mother provided. When the clock struck twelve, he toasted me and said, "I'm going to make 1981 the best year of your life." That was one promise Travis was able to keep. We kissed for a while and then settled down to watch the Johnny Carson show. He was lying on his back with my head on his chest. My legs were draped over his and I very quietly, without ceremony, said, "I love you, you know."

He turned me toward him and looked at me with serious sky-blue eyes and said, "Do you really mean it?"

"I mean it more than I've ever meant anything in my life," I replied. He held me for a long time then and kept saying over, and over "God, I love you so much." When he took me home around two a.m., I remember thinking that I was the luckiest girl alive.

Chapter Three

Travis came over to my house the next day, New Year's Day. My mother was cooking the traditional Southern New Year's Day meal, turnip greens and black-eyed peas. In the South, it is said that if you eat turnip greens on that day, then you will have lots of paper money that year. The black-eyed peas represent coins. The more you eat, the more you will prosper that year, or so the story goes.

We were sitting at the dinner table while my mom cleared the dishes, and he asked me, "What do you think the people at school will think when they find out that we're dating?" School was to resume in a few days and neither one of us was looking forward to the separation. Travis and I didn't have one class together and we ate lunch at different times, so we were looking at a full eight hours a day that we would be apart.

"I really don't care," I replied in answer to his question. "But I'm sure they're going to be shocked." Little did he know, that during Christmas vacation, I had coerced my mother into taking me shopping for jeans and flannel shirts, the official cowgirl wardrobe. I would never purchase a hat, but was known to wear one of his on occasion. When I appeared in my new clothes on the first day of school, my friends took me aside and said "WHAT are you wearing?" The last time they had seen me I was wearing dresses and funky kind of clothes, bright blue pants with a big white shirt with maybe an orange or yellow belt, big earrings, and high heels. I looked like a totally different person. Tara spoke up and said, "She started dating Travis Tritt. She met him over winter break and they started going together." ("Going together" was our way of saying going steady.) My friends were appalled, to say the least.

" Not the country-western guy?" said one girl.

"That's the one," said Tara. "Oh, God! Have you lost your mind? He's so nerdy and weird. What on earth are you thinking?" they said. In a patient voice, I explained "I'm thinking that I'm in love with him." That would pretty much be the end of my so-called friendships. If they couldn't accept him, then they couldn't accept me. Besides, I didn't need friends, I had Travis. The first couple of months at school were pretty hectic. We met each other in the halls or at my locker between classes as much as we could. Once, a teacher had to pry us away from each other. There was no kissing allowed in school, but that didn't stop us. We couldn't help it. As I look back on it now, even the teachers seemed to cut us some slack. It was almost as though they knew that we were really in love. We would write each other love notes, swap them in the hall, and read them when we got to class. It was a constant reminder of the love that we shared. We saw each other every night after school, and we spent the entire weekend together every weekend. I do remember several phone "conversations" that we had during this time. He would call and ask what I was doing. "Thinking about you" was my usual answer. And then... nothing. We wouldn't speak. We would spend hours on the phone just listening to each other breathe. I know that it sounds silly, but that's what we did. We just wanted to be connected somehow, even if it was through a telephone wire. His parents reconciled shortly after we started dating, and his mother moved back into the house that Travis grew up in. It was an old brick ranch style house that was at least 25 or 30 years old. It was a dark, depressing house with all hardwood floors, sitting back from the main road in the midst of a heavily wooded area. I remember the day that Travis first introduced me to his father. I was there for the first of what was to become the weekly Sunday dinner at his house. James was older, much older, than my father. He had married Gwen when he was 28, so he would have been in his early fifties at that time. He was wearing jeans, a black Harley-Davidson T-shirt, and a black biker's cap. He had longish hair and a grey "Z Z Top." He appeared to be missing a few teeth as well. When Travis introduced me, he almost grunted and turned back to watch the television. Travis shrugged his shoulders as if to say "What can I say?" Travis' father was a bit eccentric. He would buy most of his clothes at Sears. He loved Sears. He would find a shirt that he liked, buy five or six of them, and never wear them. They would just hang in the closet with the price tags still on them. He never appeared to buy just one of anything. Travis showed me a pocket knife that James had purchased and he had not one, but six of them. The odd thing about all of this was that he never seemed to use any of these things. Their bedroom was piled high with items that he had purchased and never used. He drove a school bus for a living, while Gwen worked as a temp for a local agency. Travis told me that they had enough money that neither of them had to work. I always thought that they did it to avoid having to be together 24 hours a day. They had a strange relationship. He was very dominating and she was subservient.

Travis once told me a story of when he was young, maybe nine or ten years old, when his dad was in a rage and was chasing after him. His mom was trying to stop James, and she deterred him long enough for Travis to make it back to his bedroom and lock the door. Travis said that he grabbed a gun that he had in his room and was afraid of what would happen if his dad came through the door. Another time, Travis had a puppy. His dad got mad at him, went outside and repeatedly kicked the puppy as hard as he could with Travis standing helplessly by. You could tell that Gwen lived her life trying to pacify James. Gwen had a big family—lots of brothers and sisters and nieces and nephews. During holidays and at lots of other times during the year, we all got together to share good food and good company. James never attended one of these gatherings that I can recall. It was a constant sore spot with Gwen. I liked Travis's mother very much, and I eventually grew to love her—I just felt sorry for her, having to live her life with a man like James. She was very meek and soft-spoken and had a good Christian heart. I felt she really supported the relationship that Travis and I were trying to build. Travis and his mom shared a special bond, and she always supported his musical ambitions. His dad, on the other hand, never thought that Travis would make it in the music industry and wanted him to get a "real job". James was very money-conscious, and worried that Travis wouldn't be able to support himself. Even though James went on those bizarre shopping trips, he usually hoarded his money like a miser. I remember once after we had gotten engaged when James said to Travis, "The only reason that she wants to marry you is so that she can get part of the money that you will inherit when I die." As if I was really going to marry someone whom I didn't love and stay married to him for 30 or 40 years, just so that I could get an inheritance! That just goes to show you how suspicious and mistrusting this man was. Despite the obvious family difficulties, my relationship with Travis flourished. Travis was able to teach me something that my father had been trying to teach me for two years—how to drive a straight shift. One cold winter's day, he took me to a nearby subdivision that had several steep hills, found the steepest one and drove halfway up it, made me get behind the wheel, and patiently taught me how to depress the clutch and shift manually. We were in the Rambler and it had a three-speed on the steering column, so it was fairly difficult to do. I desperately wanted to please him, and I spent hours learning how to change gears smoothly. He was so proud when I finally succeeded, and my dad was eternally grateful to be let off the teaching hook. This would be the beginning of the obsessive need I felt to please Travis. Sometime during the first couple of months of 1981, Travis managed to purchase a new Ford pick-up truck—just like the one in the video for "Here's a Quarter". How he loved that truck! It had a three-speed on the steering column like the Rambler and whenever we rode in it together, he would drive with his left hand and lay his right arm on the seat behind my shoulders. I would sit snuggled up next to him, and learned to shift gears with my left hand while he drove. He never shifted the gears when I was with him—that was *my* job.

After we graduated from high school, he kept his "class of 81" tassel hanging from the rear-view mirror and his pistol in the glove compartment. He had had the truck for less than two months when we were involved in a serious accident. We were hanging out at my house that night, and my parents talked us into driving down to the local Dairy Queen to get ice cream for everyone. It was only about a six-mile round trip, so we expected to be gone only a few minutes. It wound up taking hours. We were on our way home, about two miles from my house. We were on a five-lane strip, two lanes each way and a center turning lane. We were traveling at about 45 or 50 miles per hour when a Datsun 280 Z pulled out of a parking lot on our right and shot into our lane. The truck went right up over its hood, rolled off, slid across three lanes of oncoming traffic, and slammed into the curb in front of a Taco Bell, narrowly missing a head-on collision with a telephone pole. Neither one of us was wearing a seat belt. I had ice cream cones in both hands and several cups of ice cream on the seat between us, so there was ice cream and chocolate sauce all over the inside of the cab. On impact, I was thrown forward and to the side, and finally landed on the passenger side floorboard. As I lay dazed and frightened, I heard Travis groaning above me. The very first words out of his mouth were "My truck, my new truck!" I remember that I thought "Hey, what about me? You don't even know if I'm okay and you're worried about your stupid truck?" Never underestimate the love a cowboy has for his truck. We both escaped serious injury, as did the teenage guy that was driving his father's 280 Z. There was, however, a funny part to the story. I called my parents to come and get us, and ironically enough my dad drove a 280 Z just like the one we'd hit. When the teenager's father arrived, he saw my dad's car first and came running over with a look of relief on his face. "Oh thank God!" he said. "It doesn't even look like it's been in a wreck!" My dad said "This is my car. Your car is over there." The man's face crumpled when he saw his car with the whole front end smashed. Travis's truck was totaled, and he was able to get a brand new one just like it.

Chapter Four

On March 13, 1981, my family suffered a crisis that took us out of town for three weeks. Travis and I were both devastated at the long separation that was being imposed upon us. Even though it was going to be emotionally rough for a while, Travis was very kind and gracious to me and my family during this difficult period. He offered to follow my parents to the airport, and let me ride with him so that we could stall the farewell as long as possible. The trip took about an hour, and I cried and clung to him the entire time. As I was boarding the plane, I turned around for one last look at him. He had tears welling up in his eyes and I felt like my heart was breaking. Three weeks might as well have been three years. I didn't know how I was going to survive without him. In retrospect, I wonder how our love could have grown so strong in just three short months. I'm sure the flight attendants were worried about me, because I continued to cry throughout the entire flight. Much later, Travis told me that he had cried on his way back to Marietta. The time dragged on, but finally we flew back to Atlanta. Upon our return, we drove to a friend's cabin on a local lake to stay for a little while. I called Travis as soon as I could, and he immediately started on the thirty-minute drive to the lake. I was watching out the window for him to arrive, and as soon as I saw the truck I rushed out the door, ready to fling myself into his arms. I stopped short when I saw his hair. During the numerous telephone conversations that I'd had with him during my family-imposed, three-week exile, he had neglected to inform me that he'd been to the salon and gotten a perm. Not just a body wave, a curly perm. He looked like Bozo the Clown. I decided not to say anything to him at that point, because I couldn't think of a nice way to tell him that he looked ridiculous. Besides, it didn't matter. I was home! I could actually hold him and feel him and kiss him, all the things I'd been dying to do for three weeks. We went inside and talked for hours. We never let each other go. After that, we never spent one day apart until April 1984. Travis had started a contemporary Christian band that he called "Prince of Peace" shortly before I left to go out of town. We were out on the deck of the lake house one day when Travis discovered that I too could sing. He was playing his guitar and singing one of the gospel songs that he had written. Since I had inherited my mother's natural ability to sing harmony, I started singing along with him. He stopped playing, walked over to me, and said, "Sing a little louder so that I can hear you." "I don't want to," I replied. "I can't sing nearly as well as you can, and I'm embarrassed."

"But it sounds good. Please... just try it once for me." he pleaded. He started playing again. I took a deep breath and shakily joined him in singing the song. It got easier and felt better as we got going. Our voices blended very well together. When we were through, he laughed and hugged me and said "You have a great voice! You can be in the band with me! Can you do this in front of a congregation?"

"I guess so, just as long as we practice a lot before I do!" I said. We ran through a few more songs that afternoon, with Travis singing melody and me trying to pick out the harmony. Some of the songs were difficult to harmonize with, and he patiently helped me work through them. Travis had written several very touching Christian songs during that time. "I'm your Father... you're my Son" was one of the better ones. It never failed to make a church full of people cry. "Start a Fire" was another good one. In that one, Travis is praying to

God to "start a fire" in his soul and make him strive to read the Bible and become a better Christian. Travis obviously played the guitar in the band, and he was the only singer until I joined. His cousin Daryl played the bass guitar and another older cousin, Mike, played the drums. We had a few rehearsals together and started playing youth concerts at local churches. My family was still at the lake house and Travis and I were aching to be alone together, so we devised a plan to sneak away for a couple of days. We told our parents that we were scheduled to play a youth concert in Waycross, a little town in southern Georgia. We told them that it was a three-day tent revival and that we would be staying at the home of one of the church members. All of this was a lie. Travis and I went alone to St. Augustine, Florida, a very small town on the eastern coast of Florida just over the state line. We checked into a cheap hotel right on the beach, and it was in this hotel room that Travis lost his virginity. Earlier in our relationship, he had explained to me that he had never been with a woman in an intimate way. We were in the kitchen, and somehow the conversation had turned to sex. He asked me if I was a virgin and I said "Well, not exactly." In March of 1980, when I was sixteen years old, I had a boyfriend named Ricky who was a jock at a rival school. After dating for three months, I lost my virginity on his waterbed while listening to a Bruce Springsteen album. We had sex two or three times, then I caught him in bed with another girl and broke up with him. Shortly thereafter, in a form of immature teenage revenge, I had sex with his best friend, just to make him mad. It didn't work, and I just felt all the worse for it. I would not go to bed with anyone else until I made love with Travis on April 12, 1981. After telling my story, I asked Travis about his experiences. He blushed three shades of red and hemmed and hawed. Hanging his head, he admitted that he never had. I'm sure my face registered my surprise, but inside I was secretly pleased. It's not often that you meet an eighteen-year-old virgin, especially a guy. "Well, it's nothing to be ashamed of," I replied. "I think it's really neat." The subject was not brought up again until we were in the motel room in Florida. We had been dating for four and a half months, had declared undying love for each other, and had swapped class rings. The natural next step was to consummate our love in a physical way. After a long romantic walk on the beach at sunset, we called our parents from a pay phone near the hotel lobby and told them of our safe arrival in "Waycross". We also told them that the couple we were staying with didn't have a phone, so we would call them every day so they wouldn't worry. We went back to the room and decided to take a shower... together. This would be a first for both of us. I was very modest when it came to my body. I quickly undressed. Trying to suck in my tummy and make my rear end somehow look five inches smaller, I jumped into the shower. Travis soon followed me. We stood shyly looking at each other for awhile. During the previous months, we'd made it to "first base" and "second base", but had never seen each other totally nude. It was awkward at first, but after we started kissing passion washed away all feelings of ineptitude. Travis washed my hair, which I thought was very sexy. After we got out of the shower and wrapped up in ordinary white hotel towels, we made our way cautiously to the bed. We were both extremely nervous, Travis because this would be the first time, and me because it had been a year since my last encounter, I wasn't at all experienced, and I had never been with someone that I loved as deeply as Travis. We both lay down on the bed on our backs, not touching or saying anything. As the clock ticked on, I started shaking in my nervousness. Not just trembling a little on the inside, I was downright shuddering. Travis leaned over, looked at me with all seriousness, and said, "Did you put a quarter in the bed?" I started laughing and that seemed to ease the tension a bit. Before long we were kissing. Our excitement started to rise, and we began to make love. We were very inept and clumsy, but it was also a very sweet and touching experience. In the previous months, his slow passionate kisses had awakened a fire in me that I didn't even know existed. He was so incredibly sexy. Even though he was inexperienced, he instinctively knew what to do. In the midst of our act of love, I felt so connected to him, as if our souls had somehow touched. I have never since, felt that feeling with anyone else in my life, not in 31 years. It was one of the most magical moments I've ever experienced. I've never forgotten it.

We fell asleep in each other's arms, and made love again upon awakening the next morning. I don't remember exactly how many times we had sex in those three days, but I'm sure it was excessive. We couldn't get enough of each other. We were insatiable, not just for the physical pleasure, but for the emotional bonding as well. The more we made love, the deeper our love became. Travis quickly became an expert at reading my body and would do his utmost to bring me pleasure. My body soon became as satisfied as my heart and soul. He took care of my every need. We didn't use birth control that weekend, but we did talk about it. We decided that I would go on the Pill as soon as we returned home. Neither one of us were ready to become parents, and we thought that we were being very mature to make such a decision when so many of our peers were having unprotected sex. When it was time to leave the beach, we packed our few things and climbed into the truck. We felt a closeness on the return trip that had not been there on the way down. If I had simply loved Travis before, I worshipped him after our shared intimacy. I have never felt as close to a man as I did with Travis. I had opened up to him completely ,and in doing so dramatically altered the course of my life. He would become the barometer against which I would measure all future loves. I have fallen in love with two men since Travis and have said the same thing about them both: "I love him, but not in the way that I loved Travis." No one ever could or will take his place in my heart. My emotions were overwhelming as we left our St. Augustine hideaway. I remember Travis wore jeans, his straw hat, and no shirt, because the truck didn't have air conditioning and it was hot. I lay down in the front seat, put my head in his lap, and just gazed at him with all the love I had shining through my eyes. At one point,

I sat in his lap as he held me with one arm and drove with the other, while I laid my head on his chest and kissed his neck and nibbled his ear.

Travis was a big fan of the Burt Reynolds movie "Smokey and the Bandit." At one time in that movie, Sally Field rode in Burt Reynolds' lap while he drove a black Trans-Am. Travis thought it would be fun it we did that. We finally made it home, and life pretty much returned to normal. We still had a few more weeks of school to get through before graduation. Due to my family's crisis, I had missed a few weeks and had some catching up to do.

I did, however, manage to find time to schedule an appointment with a doctor to get a prescription for birth control pills. A girl at school had told me that he would put teenagers on the Pill without their parents' permission. I could have told my mom about my situation because we had that kind of relationship, but I just wanted to be mature and handle it on my own. The visit was going to cost about $100, and somehow, Travis came up with the money. He even went with me to the appointment for moral support. The visit went fine, but I had forgotten about the routine Pap smear. The results are mailed to you a few weeks later. One afternoon, I walked into the house and my mom said that I had received some mail. She had a rather icy tone in her voice that I didn't recognize until I saw what she was referring to. There was an envelope from the doctor. "Oops!" I thought as I took the envelope and started back to my room. My mother intercepted me and said "Well?" in a demanding voice.

"Well, what?" I replied nervously.

"Are you or aren't you?" she said.

"Am I or am I not WHAT?" I replied thoroughly confused.

"PREGNANT!" she said in exasperation.

"NO!" I said in horror. "Whatever gave you that idea?"

She just pointed to the envelope that was still clutched in my sweaty hand. "Oh God, Mom, no. I'm just on the Pill and this is my Pap smear report." It was a little like the old joke about the guy who tells his parents that he's dying, and after their shocked exclamations and obvious dismay says "I'm only kidding... I'm just gay." We never spoke about it after that, but years later she told me how proud she was that I had taken such a responsible step. Our Senior Prom was approaching at the end of May. I was excited to be going with the Senior that I loved. I borrowed a dress, cream-colored with a little lace jacket from Tara. When Travis told me that he was going to Gingiss Formal Wear to reserve his tuxedo, I offered to go with him. Secretly, I wanted to make sure that he picked one that would match my dress. He assured me that he had everything under control, and I let him go alone to the mall. This was a colossal mistake on my part. The next night was prom night. I got dressed and waited for Travis to arrive. When he walked through the front door, I nearly died. He had rented a chocolate-brown velvet tuxedo! In 1981! Velvet had been out of date for at least ten years. I felt sure that some guy at the formal wear shop was having a tremendous laugh at Travis' expense, but there was nothing to be done. I had no choice but to go with him to the Prom in his velvet tuxedo and hope that it was dark enough that no one would notice. The dance was being held at an exclusive country club in the suburbs of Atlanta. It was fairly uneventful. I do remember feeling awfully proud when it came time for the Senior Walk. The couples walked alone down a red carpet under a spotlight while the announcer called our names. I just beamed when he said "Travis Tritt and his date, Karen Binette." After the Prom, we went back to my parents' house. My mother had prepared a midnight breakfast for us and our friends, complete with champagne. Several couples came back with us, including my twin brother Kevin and his girlfriend Sandra. We had a great time at the midnight party and Travis spent the night on the sofa. He had had a little too much champagne, and my folks didn't want him to drive home. They offered everyone at the party a place to sleep if they didn't feel that they were able to drive home safely. My parents were really cool. The Prom and the party had been a total success, thanks to my parents.

Graduation day loomed, and I would later be thankful that I had managed to go to Florida in April because Travis absolutely refused to let me make the Seniors' annual trek to Daytona Beach after graduation. After the ceremony on June 6, 1981, we all went over to a friend's house for a post-graduation party being given by her parents. There were probably thirty or forty graduates at the function, including my brother Kevin. Travis and I mingled for a while, then I left him to go talk with my old "gang". The girls seemed glad to see me, but immediately started trying to talk me into going to Daytona with them. "Come on... it will be a blast. Everybody is going. All Seniors do this every June. It won't be the same without you," they implored. Travis and I hadn't really discussed the trip—I just assumed that I wouldn't go, but my friends made it sound like so much fun that I decided to talk to him about it, which was a big mistake. He got very angry and told me that there was no way his girlfriend was going to "run off to Florida to act like some slutty single girl." I was appalled. I had never seen him react this way before. It didn't take long for my obsessive need to please him to kick in, and I was apologizing to him for even bringing it up. My brother Kevin had overheard both conversations and subsequently told my father that Travis was refusing to allow me to go on the trip. My dad pulled me aside and said "Honey, if you want to go, then go. Don't let Travis tell you what you can or can't do. If you let him get away with this now, you'll set a pattern for the rest of your relationship. I think that you should go, and I'll even pay for it. You're only young once."

"But, Dad," I said. "I can't go if he won't let me. If I do go, then he'll be furious with me and I can't stand that." "I think you are making a big mistake," said my father. "You are already letting him dictate to you what you can or can't do. You're headed for trouble." "I love him, Daddy," I replied passionately. "What else can I do?" I turned and walked back to Travis. I wanted to talk to him and reassure him that I wouldn't go, and reassure myself that he wasn't still angry with me. So much for Graduation Day. Even though I missed the Senior trip due to Travis, he made up for it that September.

Chapter Five

Summer was slow, lazy, and uneventful. June, July and August are steaming hot sweltering months in Georgia. The humidity gets very high, and you begin to perspire as soon as you step outside. We spent as much time in the air-conditioned indoors as possible. We continued playing in the band on a regular basis. There was an old Pentecostal church about 25 minutes from Marietta where went two or three times a week for rehearsals. We had managed to purchase a fairly modest sound system, which we carried in the back of Travis's truck. We had to load and unload the microphones, speakers, mike stands, and yards of wires frequently.

My eighteenth birthday arrived on June 11th. Travis surprised me with a burgundy, leatherbound Ryrie Study Bible. This was a nice but rather unremarkable gift except for one small detail... my name was engraved on the front in elegant gold script. I literally sat down and cried when I saw it. Travis had directed the engravers to inscribe my name as "Karen Tritt", not "Karen Binette". I just hugged him and cried harder. He never said anything such as "You know what this means, don't you?" or "Was it okay that I did that?" It was silently understood by us both. We knew exactly what this meant without actually speaking the words, and that it was more than okay. At our next rehearsal, Travis's cousin Daryl saw my new Bible and raised his eyebrows in an unspoken question, but no one ever commented about it. Daryl was a good-looking young man from a small north Georgia community called Dawsonville. He was our age and he had a twin sister named Sharon, so he and I instantly had something in common. Travis and Daryl were best friends who grew up together and just happened to be related. He was our constant sidekick once I began singing in the band. You would think that Travis and I would not want anyone to infringe on our relationship because we were so close, but Daryl was special. I loved him as much as Travis did, and I never once felt that he was cramping our style. Daryl had a great sense of humor, and was very modest and shy. When we played at youth concerts, it was Daryl who drove the teenage girls wild, not Travis. Believe me, I was a very jealous girlfriend, and I was on the lookout for that type of thing. I remember one episode that still embarrasses me to this day. Travis had an acquaintance named Cindy who had a very beautiful voice. She was an active youth member in her church. She had been asked to sing in a friend's wedding, and the song that the bride chose was a duet. Cindy needed a singing partner, so she naturally called Travis. Since Travis had performed in numerous weddings, he readily agreed. I was fine until we got to the church for rehearsal. As soon as I saw them standing up there together singing a love song, I saw red or green or whatever the color is associated with EXTREME jealousy. It hit me like a lead ball in my stomach! I hated having to watch another girl sing with MY boyfriend—I was the only one who was supposed to sing with him. I had to get up and leave the sanctuary. Later that night as we were driving home, I cried and pleaded with him to understand the intensity of my emotion. Needless to say, he didn't understand, and in my reexamination of that night, I really can't say that I blame him. No man could have understood how I felt—like the breath had been knocked out of me, so severely that I went into the bathroom and became physically ill. Though I never was to experience jealousy like that again during our relationship, I was still exceedingly jealous and protective. I'm sure that this was difficult for Travis to live with. I wanted to be with him every minute of every day. If he went into the kitchen, I went into the kitchen. If he went outside, I went outside. In retrospect, I must have driven Travis crazy with my absolute dependence on him. If we were at a club where he was performing and the women were openly flirting with him, I would walk up to Travis and take his hand possessively as if to say "he's mine...back off!" I wanted him all to myself.

The friend's wedding went smoothly, and I was able to contain myself during the ceremony by saying over and over to myself "It's just a song... no big deal." Even though my behavior was childish and immature, Travis tried to make me feel better by taking me on a trip to Helen, Georgia, in September of that year. Helen is a little "Swiss Alps" village in the heart of the north Georgia mountains. Travis's father owned about a hundred acres of land in White County, which is just north of Helen. Travis wanted me to see the property, so we took a weekend trip. The land was picturesque, with rolling pasture, a wooded forest, an enormous old barn with cows grazing nearby, and a river running through a portion of the acreage. We took a picnic lunch and sat eating on a large group of rocks overlooking the Chattahoochee River. When lunch was through, Travis persuaded me to make love with him on the rocks. When I voiced my doubts, he assured me that the property was deserted, that he had locked the gate behind us when we came in, and that no one would discover us. I reluctantly gave in, and we had our first outdoor sexual experience. It was warm and sunny, a beautiful September day with not a cloud in sight. Our experience was memorable, and I remember thinking that all was right with the world.

Night was falling, so we returned to our hotel room. We dressed for dinner, then ate at a unique little eatery on the main strip. Somehow, Travis managed to get a gigantic bottle of red wine, and we took it back to our room. He poured me a glass, and I took it out onto a back balcony which overlooked the river. Travis walked outside carrying his ever-present guitar. He settled down in the chair next to me and we started to sing. We stayed there for hours. When we were through, our voices were hoarse, the wine was gone, and I was more than a little tipsy. I had consumed the entire bottle by myself! Travis hated wine, so he just drank soda. I didn't realize how intoxicated I was until I started to get up. I fell back in my chair giggling. He picked me up and carried me to the nearest of the two double beds that were in the room. That's the last I remember until I woke up sometime in the middle of the night. I was sick and had apparently been so for a while, because the bed and I were both covered. The commotion woke Travis and he quickly came to my rescue. He picked me up yet again and carried me to the bathroom. Although I was still quite inebriated, I can recall that he put me in the shower and washed my hair and body, dried me off, put some clean clothes on me, and laid me down in the clean bed. Then he quietly rinsed off all the stained bedclothes in the shower and hung them up in the bathroom to dry. I asked him the next morning why he went to all that trouble and he replied, "I didn't think it was fair to have the maid do that sort of thing. I love you. It's my job to take care of you whether you are drunk or sober". I punched him in the arm, gave him a hug, and we checked out of the hotel.

When we arrived back in Marietta, we received a phone call from Jerry and Christine. Her parents were going out of town, and she wanted to have a few of us over for a little party. We agreed to go, but I told Travis ahead of time that I was not going to drink. At that point, I didn't care if I ever saw a bottle of wine again. The gathering was to be a small one, Travis and me, Jerry and Christine, and three other couples. We were in the living room, just sitting around drinking beer and soda, when the doorbell rang. Christine answered the door and was surprised to find ten or twelve people from school standing on the doorstep of her parents' house. "Is this where the party is?" said one guy. "What party are you talking about?" asked Christine. "The big party that everyone's talking about," said the guy as he shouldered his way into the house. Apparently, word had gotten around that a party was happening at Christine's and groups of people started crashing the party. There is an invisible radar that all teenagers hone in on that tells them when and where a party is happening. The radar seems to grow more intense if the party is in an adult's house without his or her permission. Before long, the house was filled with sixty or seventy people who had brought beer and were making an incredible amount of noise. We knew things were getting out of control when someone broke a coffee table or some other piece of furniture. Travis and Jerry and the other guys who were in the original group decided to take matters into their own hands. They went through the crowded house, politely asking people to leave, but the drunk and rowdy mob was oblivious to their requests. Jerry started telling folks that the neighbors had called the police due to the excessive noise. That piece of information at least got them moving towards the door. Finally, the house was empty except for the original ten of us. We thought the ordeal was over until a huge rock came flying through the plate glass window on the front side of the house. Jerry flung open the door while Christine stared in horror at the broken window, no doubt trying to decide how she was going to explain THIS to her parents. The crowd was milling around the front lawn of the house. They had evidently waited around to see if the police were indeed going to show up. When they realized that they had been tricked, they got angry and started throwing things at the house. Jerry was furious, but he alone was no match for all those intoxicated party crashers. He got into a fistfight with the rock thrower, and that started a brawl. All of a sudden, our dates ran out of the house and started fighting in the front yard.

It was very dark and extremely difficult to see what was happening. I had no idea if Travis was safe. I stood shaking on the front porch, peering into the night, trying to find him among all the fighting. Suddenly, someone fired a pistol into the air and everyone scattered. In a few moments, only our boyfriends were left standing on the lawn. I ran down the steps and flung myself into Travis' arms, trying to look everywhere at once to make sure he was unharmed. He appeared to be fine—his clothes and hair were messy, but otherwise he was okay. I was tremendously relieved. Physical violence has always terrified me, and I was so glad that Travis was able to take care of himself in the midst of the brawl.

It was shortly after this episode that Travis and I decided to get jobs. College was never an option for either one of us, and our parents were tired of funding our little adventures. Sometime that fall, Travis began work as a warehouse employee for Dealer's Supply Company in Marietta, a small heating and air conditioning business. I worked as a cashier at a Burger King restaurant just down the street. He would work for Dealer's Supply for at least two and a half years, while I worked at Burger King for four months until another job became available that enabled me to use the medical office training that I had acquired while working at the orthopedic practice my mother managed. We hated the separation, but knew that we had to earn a living in order to begin our new life together. Though Travis hated Burger King food, he spent every lunch hour there for four months, eating double Whoppers with cheese and onion rings just so he could see me. He actually made very little money working in the warehouse, but he was able to save enough to buy me an engagement ring.

Chapter Six

The holiday season was soon upon us. Travis and I were preparing to make the annual drive to North Georgia to spend Thanksgiving with his family. The feast was held every year in the trailer where his maternal grandparents lived. "Nanny" and "Papa" were two of the nicest people I had ever had the pleasure of meeting. Papa was a Pentecostal preacher who would marry us the following year. Nanny was the true matriarch of the family, and she ruled with a firm hand and a loving heart. Both attributes would serve her well as a minister's wife. Gwen (Travis' mother) had several siblings, and when we all got together there was usually a crowd. It was difficult for all of us to fit into the trailer at one time, but we did it because it seemed important to Nanny that we come to her home at least once a year. We usually went during Thanksgiving, because after the wonderful meal, the men would get their rifles and go deer hunting. Travis almost always stayed behind, as hunting did not appeal to him. On this particular Thanksgiving, Travis and Sheilah and I were driving to the mountains in the truck. This would be the day when I would see Travis' unleashed temper for the first time. We were on a mountain road, far away from anywhere, when something happened to the truck and the engine suddenly died. We pulled off to the side of the road and Travis started getting angry. He got out to inspect the truck and to see if he could determine the problem. After a few minutes of investigation, Sheilah and I heard him shouting and cursing and then he started kicking the tires of the truck as hard as he could. I was shocked at his outburst, but Sheilah acted as though this was all too familiar to her. I couldn't believe he was actually kicking his beloved truck! Somehow the problem was resolved, and after about an hour's delay we were on our way once again. There was a good bit of tension in the truck after Travis' little eruption, but I didn't dare say anything to him about it. I never told him how much it scared me to see him totally lose control of his temper that day. I promised myself that I would never do anything to cause him to react in that manner toward me. Travis was still a little angry when we arrived at the trailer, but the holiday progressed as usual despite his dark mood. We ate too much, caught up on aunts and uncles and cousins, and generally enjoyed ourselves. I made it a point to be especially accommodating to Travis that day in order to improve his mood as much as I could. I made his plate for him, piled high with his favorite foods: turkey and dressing, fresh green beans out of a relative's garden, his mother's homemade pickles, and his favorite dessert, Magic Cookie Bars, a dessert popular in the South, similar to a coconut, fudge, brownie concoction. I carried the food and a glass of sweetened iced tea outside so he wouldn't have to be bothered with serving himself. That action was the beginning of a bad habit, and I would continuously serve Travis from then on. After that, I don't think he ever prepared his own food as long as we were together.

Christmas was getting closer, and I wanted to get Travis something really special. One day, we were in a music store and Travis was admiring a Westbury guitar. I didn't know too much about guitars and still don't to this day, but he seemed to be enraptured with this particular instrument. The price tag said $600. He knew that this was way out of his price range, but he still stopped by the store on occasion just to play it. Because he was an excellent musician, the owners of the store would let him sit and play for hours. After one session, I took Travis outside and told him that I had managed to save some money and could give him $400 toward the guitar. I told him that I had wanted to buy him some new clothes and maybe some country music albums for Christmas, but that I knew he really wanted the Westbury. I gave him the money, and he purchased the guitar the next week. He was so happy, and it thrilled me to have been able to do that for him. Christmas morning finally arrived. I jumped out of bed and ran down the hall to get my brothers.

We had a wonderful Christmas at my house that year. We all received extravagant gifts such as televisions and stereos and our own telephones. I didn't realize at the time that this would be the last Christmas that we would spend together as a family. My parents divorced the next year.

That afternoon, I went over to Travis' house. I exchanged gifts with his parents and sister. I took my high school class ring back from Travis and gave it to Sheilah. She was a freshman at Walton High School, and she wanted to borrow my ring to wear to school so everyone would think she was a senior. As evening fell, Travis asked me if I wanted to go for a drive. He had a mischievous glint in his eye, so I had an idea where he wanted to go and what he wanted to do.

After James and Gwen remarried, she left her house completely intact. It was still furnished as it had been when Travis and I first met, including the master bedroom. Travis still had his key to the house, and when the mood struck, we would drive over and spend an hour or so making love in the bed upstairs. Because all of the utilities had been turned off when they officially moved out, there was no heat or electricity. The house was very dark and extremely cold, but within minutes of our arrival at the house, Travis was able to warm me up. He would kiss me hungrily on the mouth, then move down to my neck. Sometimes, when he really wanted to drive me wild, he would move behind me and kiss the back of my neck. Then he would slowly move down and kiss me lightly down my back, tracing my spine with his lips. He enjoyed this as much as I did because he knew what kind of effect it was having on me. He could be very creative when the mood struck him. That particular night, after making love for several hours, we went downstairs into the living room. I was sitting on the couch basking in the afterglow of wonderful sex. There was a street light just in front of the house, and the glow from it illuminated the living room. Travis was being very quiet, and when he finally looked at me I could see that he was crying. "What's wrong," I asked in a soft bewildered voice. "Have I done something?"

He shook his head as tears coursed down his cheeks. He walked over to where I was sitting, knelt down in front of me, and pulled a little velvet box out of his pocket. "I love you so much," he said, his voice breaking with emotion. "I want you to marry me—will you be my wife?" I opened the box with shaking hands. Inside was a small, pear-shaped diamond solitaire engagement ring. Though it was just slightly larger than a third of a carat, I thought it was the biggest, most beautiful ring in the world. I looked at the ring, looked at Travis, and said softly, "Of course I'll marry you. I made that decision a long time ago. I was just waiting for you to ask." Then I was crying too. We sat on the old couch and held each other. It was a little frightening, taking that next big step, but we were sure that we were doing the right thing. Later that night, I was sitting up in my bed staring at my left hand. It looked so strange to see an engagement ring there! My parents came home from a Christmas dinner at my grandparents' house. My Mom came into my room and I quickly shoved my hand underneath the covers. "Well," she said. "What did he get you for Christmas?" I took a deep breath and showed her my left hand.

"Oh, Karen," she said. "Are you sure that this is what you want?"

"Yes, Mom," I replied earnestly. "I love him and I want to spend the rest of my life with him." My mother would spend the next nine months trying to talk me out of marrying Travis, and I, like any other normal teenager, would not listen to reason. The more she tried to change my mind, the more I became convinced that this was something I had to do. My dad had very little to say about the news. I think that he was going through a difficult time in his own life and he was content to let me make my own decisions about mine. Travis' father was not at all happy about our impending marriage, but I suppose he knew that it was futile to say anything to his son. His mother seemed genuinely happy for us, and she suggested that we let "Papa" marry us. We originally had planned to get married in May of the next year, but my mother convinced me that we couldn't plan a proper wedding in five months. We moved the date into the fall of 1982. September in Georgia is absolutely heavenly, and we chose Saturday the 25th as our wedding day.

Chapter Seven

New Year's 1982 came and went, with Travis and I celebrating with pizza and champagne for the second consecutive year. That year we had real champagne instead of the non-alcoholic type. If we were adult enough to be engaged, we were adult enough to have real champagne! I quit my job at Burger King in January of 1982 because I received an offer of a position in a dermatologist's office in Sandy Springs, Georgia. The practice needed a medical assistant. I had no experience in this line of work, but they were willing to train me. Because of my lack of experience, the salary was considerably lower. It did not seem low to me at the time, for it was much more than I made as a cashier at a fast-food restaurant. I enjoyed my work there and happily informed my co-workers of my impending wedding. I felt so grown up! Travis' 19th birthday arrived on February 9, 1982. We went into a western clothing store several days before his birthday. I made the mistake of telling him that I would buy him whatever his heart desired. I was feeling generous because of the recent increase in my financial situation. He walked over to the boot section and began to admire a pair of Tony Lama eelskin boots. Even though he wore boots every day when he was not working, he had the ordinary, inexpensive type that usually cost approximately $50. This pair was $330! Needless to say, I bought him those boots for his birthday present. They were the finest ones he owned during our entire relationship. During this time, our contemporary Christian group disbanded. (The drummer, Mike, had been drinking alcohol prior to some performances, and the kids were beginning to notice.) When we sat down to discuss it, Mike said that he did not want to set a bad example for any of the teenagers who attended our concerts for inspiration and guidance. We decided to give Mike some time to get his priorities straight. Meanwhile, Travis began to play secular music again. Travis, along with Mark and Kerry, two former members of his high school band, had started playing together. Mark was an accomplished banjo player, an excellent musician, and a dear friend to both Travis and me. I loved him and thoroughly enjoyed hearing him play. I always felt that if anyone of our group made the "big time", it would be Mark rather than Travis. Even though he played exceptional country music, his real talent was bluegrass. Kerry was a good bass player with a great sense of humor and the practical joker of the group. The three of them together made quite a team, and they decided to name the band "Southern Bred". Travis was the only vocalist, and oddly enough, even though he knew of my singing abilities, he never once asked to sing in this band. That was all right with me, for my Mom and I were busy planning the wedding. Band rehearsals were every Wednesday night at Mark's parents' house in Marietta. Mark and his recent bride Kathie were expecting their first child shortly following our wedding date. Kerry's girlfriend Michelle had not yet graduated from high school. Our ages were close enough so that Kathie, Michelle, and I all had common interests and became good friends. I grew to look forward to those Wednesday nights, because I could gossip with my girlfriends while the guys rehearsed. They were a "copy band" and sang all the popular country songs of that period, with only one original. "Spend A Little Time" was always in their repertoire. They sang a lot of the Gatlin Brothers, Alabama, Hank Williams, Jr., Waylon Jennings, and Willie Nelson. Travis always thought of himself as an "outlaw". I remember him saying to me once that if he ever became famous, he would be an outlaw. To me, it was like sitting around talking about what you would do with the money if you won millions of dollars in a lottery. Yes, it could conceivably happen, but realistically, it probably won't. I was wrong.

Southern Bred began playing at small country dives around town for very low pay. I remember once when they were playing at a catfish restaurant on Highway 41 in Marietta. The guys had arrived early to set up, and we girls were to join them later. When Kathie, Michelle, and I walked in, I heard "Amanda", a Waylon Jennings song which was popular at the time. Kathie turned to me and said, "Is that Travis or the jukebox?" With absolute certainty I replied, "The jukebox." I was surprised to learn that it was the band, after all. They had become so good at copying other artists' music that even I could not tell the difference. Travis also would sing the song by Alabama, "Close Enough To Perfect," and dedicate it to me. It made me feel so good for him to publicly acknowledge me in that way. I felt so important!

We had some friends who were active in the rodeo circuit. Occasionally, a rodeo would be held at the Circle C Ranch in Alpharetta, Georgia. That spring, the band was asked to play. If you have ever been to a rodeo, then you know that music is played while a steer or a horse is being led into a holding pen. The music continues throughout the event, but as soon as the rider is thrown or the steer is roped, the music must stop instantly. Keep in mind that while I have never played a musical instrument or sung at a rodeo, it would seem to me that it would be difficult if not impossible to play well under these circumstances. The band, however, took it all in stride and did a great job. The rodeo lasted for two days. Travis and I spent the night in the hay barn. After staying up all night talking, we climbed up on top of a chicken house to watch the sunrise. We were both in need of a bath, so we drove home and met back at the ranch later that morning. (When I was eleven years old, my parents bought me a beautiful seven-year old Palomino gelding, which I rode almost daily for five years. Because of this, I considered myself to be an expert... well, adequate...rider. However, all of my "expertise" did not prevent my being thrown from a bucking horse and sustaining a severe sprain of my right ankle. My ankle was extremely painful and very swollen, badly enough that my boot had to be cut off.) I was more upset by that than the accident, for it was my only pair of cowboy boots. Most of my family came to the rodeo that day, including my grandparents, who live in Alpharetta, and my Aunt Carolyn and her family from Carrollton, Georgia. Aunt Carolyn was then, and still is, a huge fan of Travis' music. After he became famous, she contacted Gwen to ask for Travis' phone number. She has been employed by the Sony Record Corporation in Carrollton for over ten years, and Sony periodically holds an "Open House" for all of the artists on its record label. She wanted to issue an invitation to Travis. and although he was unable to attend, the phone call was not a total waste of time. She did receive an 8 X 10 glossy autographed picture of Travis! Even though my brothers Kevin and Keith were not big fans of the rodeo, they also came that day to please me. It's a good thing that the three of us were so close, because in that summer of 1982, Travis would try his best to drive a wedge between us.

Chapter Eight

The wedding was getting closer. Mom and I had to get busy. Travis' aunt owned a bridal shop in Marietta called "The Wedding Knot," and Gwen suggested that we go there to pick out my gown. His aunt was very nice and helpful. The first dress that I selected was a beautiful ivory gown trimmed in antique lace with a long train. We found a stunning bridal hat to match, and I truly looked the part of a Southern belle. There is something very romantic about choosing a wedding gown, and the entire experience felt very unreal to me. We put the dress on layaway and left the shop feeling extremely pleased with our choice. When I described the gown to Travis, he became very upset and insisted that I wear a conventional white dress with a traditional veil. No ivory dress! No hat! Period! End of discussion! I, of course, wanted to please my groom, so I returned to the shop and chose another gown more to his liking. There was only one minor problem—it wouldn't zip up the back! My mom told me that I would need to lose weight in order to fit into it. "No problem," I thought. I still had five months until the wedding. I had asked Sandra, Kevin's girlfriend, to be my maid of honor. Sheilah was to be a bridesmaid, along with Daryl's twin sister Sharon. My second cousin Rebekah, who was four at the time, would be the flower girl. We chose simple, ankle-length lilac dresses with lace jackets and matching shoes for the bride's attendants. Meanwhile, there were still a caterer, florist and photographer to choose. Our photographer was a very sweet, good-natured man named Norm Pascal. He had a wonderful reputation and was an excellent photographer. He made our engagement photograph for the Marietta Daily Journal. We were so pleased with the quality of his work that we chose him for our big day. The fee for our wedding pictures was $800, which include 72 8 x 10 prints in an engraved leather-bound album. I remember the cost because my mother still has the cancelled check. My parents were responsible for paying all of the usual and customary wedding expenses. Travis himself had to foot the bill for the rehearsal dinner, since James refused to contribute in any way to our wedding. I suppose that this was his way of expressing his displeasure. Through my mother's connections in the medical community, we were able to locate a wonderful caterer. We went to her home one afternoon to choose the cakes and set the menu for the reception. We had the traditional wedding fare, along with non-alcoholic punch. The base of the punch was grape juice, and the caterer was able to almost match the shade of the attendants' dresses. The wedding cake was a three-tiered, lemon-flavored white cake with white icing in the shape of lilacs cascading over the top and sides. Travis' groom's cake was an octagon-shaped chocolate layer cake with a basket-weave design, decorated with frosted fresh grapes. The wedding ceremony was scheduled for early evening, and we had decided upon a candlelit service. With this in mind, I chose frosted hurricane candle arrangements for my attendants. A wreath of lilacs surrounded the base of each white candle, and each had streamers of lilac and white satin ribbons. My bouquet was white roses and baby's breath with two red roses in the center. Travis and the male members of the wedding party wore boutonnieres of lilac roses and baby's breath. The tables in the church reception hall were covered with white damask tablecloths and decorated with ivy streamers and large white satin bows made by my Aunt Joyce. I was relieved when all of these decisions were final. I decided to return to the bridal shop to try on my dress again. About six weeks had passed, and we were at the beginning of June—time was running short. I had indeed lost a few pounds, and was confident that the dress would fit. When I arrived at the shop and tried it on, it still would not zip up completely. I removed the gown, determined to starve myself for the next four months if that's what it took! My mom made me return periodically to check my progress. We eventually discovered that although the tag on the outside of the gown stated it was a size 10, it was actually a size 8! There wasn't time for an alteration, so I had to choose another dress in the correct size. I was very happy with the final selection, and surprisingly, so was Travis. I looked like a traditional bride. During this time, even though I had not spoken directly to Travis about it, I assumed that my brothers Kevin and Keith would be groomsmen. It is traditional to have the siblings of the bride and groom in the wedding party, and since Travis had already asked Sheilah to be a bridesmaid, I had already brought up the subject to my brothers. They were pleased that I had thought to include them in our big day. During one of our many discussions concerning wedding preparations, I casually mentioned to Travis that I had asked them to be in the wedding. He literally exploded! "This is MY wedding too and I will decide who I want as my groomsmen! I DO NOT want your BROTHERS in my wedding! Daryl is going to be my best man, and Mark and Jerry are going to be my attendants," he said.

In a rare show of courage, I said, "But Travis, they're my brothers! They're *supposed* to be in the wedding. Besides, I've already invited them to be in the ceremony!"

"Well, you can just UN-invite them! This is MY wedding too, and I'm going to have some say in how things are done!" I was very hurt and did not understand how he could be so cold. In the past, Travis had been warm and generous. I was truly baffled by his attitude toward my brothers. Understandably, my parents were hurt as well as angry. After all, they were paying the major portion of the wedding costs. After sitting down and trying to reason with Travis, he agreed to their being ushers. This was not really a compromise so far as my family was concerned, but it would have to do. This was the most they were going to get out of Travis. With all of the wedding plans coming together, sometimes smoothly and sometimes not, I decided to change jobs. An opportunity arose for a position with a pediatric dermatologist who had a smaller practice. I was to be one of two assistants, and I worked there when our wedding day arrived.

Chapter Nine

August is when we in Georgia typically experience the "dog days" of summer. The heat is unbearable, and everyone prays for the early arrival of autumn. This particular August, Travis and I were at his house for the Sunday dinner ritual with his parents. After the meal, I went into Travis' bedroom to lie down and take a nap. His room was the coolest in the house and I was seeking relief from the sweltering heat. I lay down on the bed and soon fell fast asleep. I was awakened by an arm around my waist and a beard nuzzling against my cheek. I turned over and said in a sleepy voice, "What are you doing? Your parents are going to walk in here any minute."

"No, they won't," he replied with a gleam in his eye. "They've taken Sheilah to play miniature golf and they won't be back for at least two hours. We have the whole house to ourselves." That was all the invitation that I needed! Within minutes, we had removed our clothes and were making passionate love on his bed. Because we were alone, we made the mistake of leaving the bedroom door open. Even though I am not a vocal lover by nature, it excited Travis for me to express myself in a rather loud voice. The episode was reaching its peak and it was getting rather noisy in the bedroom when we heard footsteps in the hallway and saw the hall light come on. We both froze! His parent's had returned unexpectedly and had caught us in the act. Even though we were getting married in less than two months, we had led them to believe that we were saving ourselves for our wedding night. We were both mortified! Travis, in an attempt to disguise what was obviously a display of passion, said in a voice loud enough for his parents to hear, "Honey, wake up! I think you're having a bad dream or something!" Had I not been so embarrassed, I would have laughed. It was such a touching attempt to delude his parents into thinking that what they heard was the nightmare-induced ravings of their son's fiance. Travis jumped up and quickly slammed the door shut. When he turned back to me, Travis had a look on his face that terrified me. He looked like the caged animals in the zoo, the ones who don't want to be there and would do anything to escape. He threw on his clothes and began to pace around the room, trying to figure his way out of this mess. There was a small window in his bedroom that might have been an adequate escape route if it had not been nailed shut some years before. When he realized that there was no way we were going to get out of that house except through the front door, he started to pound his head against the wall while muttering a certain expletive under his breath. He was obviously very frustrated and upset. I was also disturbed, but not nearly to the degree that Travis was. I guess it made sense, because after all, they were his parents. After about an hour, we took a deep breath and walked down the hall, into the living room, past his astonished parents, and out the front door. We didn't speak to them or even look at them on the way out. By this time, I was rather amused by the whole experience. However, it would take Travis a while to recover. He was still agitated about it the night that he and his groomsmen went to pick out their tuxedos. We were at Mark's parents' house, waiting for everyone to arrive. The mood was jovial and everyone seemed to realize that the choosing of formal wear signified that the wedding date was indeed drawing near. I was going to go with the guys to make sure that they chose the correct colors and style. I still remembered the prom fiasco, and I didn't want to take any chances with the most important event in my life. Just as we were about to leave, I became violently ill. The only thing that I can attribute this to is a bad case of nerves. I was so sick that I couldn't accompany them to the mall. I begged Travis to please exercise good taste in selecting his attire. My worries were needless because on our wedding day he was dressed in a beautiful, conservative dark grey tuxedo, with his groomsmen in a lighter shade of grey. Everyone looked extremely handsome, and there was not a swatch of velvet in sight! September 25th dawned clear, sunny and warm. There was not a cloud in the sky, and the temperature would not get above seventy-five degrees. It was a perfect day to get married. I woke up around nine and went into the kitchen to have coffee and call my groom. Travis had moved out of his parents' house and into our one-bedroom apartment at the beginning of September. We had his parents' cast-off furniture, as well as a beautiful solid oak round kitchen table and four chairs that Travis had bought and refinished for me as a wedding gift. He had not slept at the apartment the night before the wedding, choosing instead to spend one last night in his childhood home. Our phone conversation that morning was brief, filled with "I love you" and "I can't believe today is finally here." He ended with "I'll see you at the church. I love you more than you'll ever know." I spent the rest of the day trying not to be nervous and wondering if 11:00 a.m. was too early to start getting ready for a 7:00 p.m. wedding! Finally, it was time to begin the preparations. After I showered, applied my make-up, and fixed my hair, it was time to put on my wedding gown. Even though some brides choose to get dressed at the church, I wanted to get ready at home. My mother had arranged for me to drive to the church in a white Model-A Ford that belonged to one of the doctors that she worked for. He had graciously offered to let us borrow the car, and we happily accepted.

It was a special touch on what was already an exceptional day. My bags were already packed for my wedding night. My father and I rode in the Model-A while my mother and brothers followed behind us with my luggage in her car. The old car would only go about

15-20 miles per hour, so we had to allow enough time to get to the church about twelve miles away. I'm sure that we made quite a romantic sight as we drove down the road, me in my wedding gown and veil and my dad looking very dapper in a classic black tuxedo. People waved and honked their horns at us as we slowly made our way to the church. We spoke very little during the drive. I held hands with my dad as I stared at the royal blue velvet box in my lap which contained Travis' wedding band. I'm not sure that I truly understood the magnitude of what I was doing. I wasn't exactly nervous, but I knew in my heart that I wanted everything to be right. I wanted to be a good wife and make Travis happier than he'd ever been. I never had a moment's doubt about that day. I wanted to marry him more than anything. We arrived at the church about 5:30 p.m. Marietta Assembly of God was an elegant, contemporary church that Travis' grandfather had helped build some years before. It was fitting that he would officiate at our wedding ceremony in the very church he had helped to construct. We went inside and began the hour-long process of photographs. My attendants were already dressed and present at the church when I arrived. Following tradition, I was not allowed to see Travis before the ceremony, but I sent word with his sister that I loved him and that I couldn't wait to become Mrs. Travis Tritt. After the photographer was through taking pictures of everyone except James, we made our way to the church lobby. James refused to be in any of the photographs, but I couldn't let that bother me. I had other things on my mind. Kevin and Keith were standing at the double doors leading into the sanctuary, looking resplendent in their tuxedos. All the guests had been seated, and the time had arrived. They both hugged me and then went in to sit down. My father also hugged me, and after kissing me and telling me that he loved me, opened the door. Together, we began the journey down the aisle that would take me out of his arms and into another man's.

Chapter Ten

I have never seen my dad cry as hard or as much as he did the day that I married Travis. He started when we were walking down the aisle to the strains of "Here Comes the Bride." By the time we reached the end of the aisle, he was sobbing loudly enough for the entire church to hear. I patted his arm in understanding and stared into the crystal blue eyes of the love of my life. Before my father gave me away, Travis walked up to a small platform behind the minister and sat down in a folding chair. His guitar was already waiting for him. I knew that he was going to sing to me at our wedding, but he would never divulge the name of the song. He had decided to sing the very first song that he had ever sung to me: "Lady" by John Denver. It is a very appropriate wedding song. There is a line in the song that reads "Today our lives were joined became entwined. I wish that you could know how much I love you." That song made all one hundred and fifty wedding guests cry. There wasn't a dry eye in the house, except for mine—I don't even think my eyes got misty. Travis was so obviously moved by the raw emotion that his voice broke during the song. I still don't know why I didn't cry at my own wedding. When the song ended, Travis walked back down to where I was standing. When his grandfather asked "Who gives this woman to be married to this man?", my father had composed himself enough to give the standard reply of "Her mother and I". The wedding progressed without a flaw. Travis and I repeated our vows, substituting the word "cherish" for "obey." I may have obeyed Travis in the past and was most certainly going to continue to do so in the future, but I didn't want an entire church full of people to know about it! We exchanged rings—mine a simple, thin gold band and his a narrow, textured gold band that looked very elegant on his hand. After admonishing us to "love and protect each other until death do us part", Papa pronounced us husband and wife. The moment that he introduced "Mr. and Mrs. Travis Tritt" was truly a momentous one. I'll never forget how it felt. I was so proud to have this man as my husband. I was convinced that we would grow old and even die together in our sleep, because surely even God knew that I couldn't live without him. After beaming at the wedding guests for a few moments, we hurried down the aisle. I stopped to kiss my new mother-in-law and present her with a rose out of my bouquet, and then I turned and did the same for my own mother. When we reached the lobby, we had a few minutes to ourselves before the guests started out of the sanctuary. We hugged and kissed and stared at each other's hands. It looked so strange to see wedding rings there! It was a wonderful symbol of our newfound commitment. The reception began while Travis and I had our post-ceremony photographs taken. When we went downstairs to the church reception room, everyone cheered. We cut the cake, drank some punch, and visited with our friends and family for a little while. The hour was growing late and we were eager to get to our hotel room. We were staying at the Hilton for one night and would leave the next morning for our honeymoon in Gatlinburg, Tennessee. Since Travis did not want his truck to be decorated with the usual whipped cream, soap, toilet paper and balloons, my mom volunteered her silver Oldsmobile Cutlass. We left the reception in a shower of birdseed, then quickly jumped in the car and sped away to begin our new life together. I had no idea that another significant new life had already begun in Arkansas during our wedding ceremony. (After Travis and I arrived at the Hilton, I received a phone call from my mom. "You have another wedding present," she said playfully. "Who is it from?" I asked. "Cindy," she replied. "What is it?" I asked. "A baby boy," my mom said proudly. While Travis and I were saying "I do," my nephew Gregory was being born in a hospital just outside Little Rock, Arkansas. Keith and Cindy (Gregory's mother) had dated for a while before she moved out of state with her family. She discovered that she was pregnant shortly after they left. Though Keith and Cindy would never marry, our family would keep in constant contact with Cindy and Gregory. Travis and I had a typical wedding night, complete with all of the anticipated pleasures. I had heard stories of women who, upon awakening the morning after their wedding, think to themselves "Oh no... what have I done?" I had none of these feelings of trepidation or remorse. I was positive I had done a wonderful thing by marrying Travis, and from the look in his eyes I could tell the feeling was mutual. After a quick breakfast, we drove to my house to drop off mom's car and pick up the truck. Then we were off to Tennessee for a three-day honeymoon. We stayed at the Grand Hotel in Dolly Parton's hometown of Pigeon Forge which is on the outskirts of Gatlinburg, Tennessee. Oddly enough, I remember next to nothing about our honeymoon except for one incident. On our first night there, I wanted to eat dinner at a elegant restaurant overlooking the river. There was about an hour's delay for a table, and I was willing to wait. After all, we had dressed for a nice dinner and I was in no hurry. Travis obviously was feeling the need to rush because he refused to wait, and we wound up eating chopped hamburger patties in a cheesy little place called Johnny's Diner. I was mortified at his behavior. It seemed to me that he acted as if the maitre d' at the expensive restaurant should have materialized a table out of thin air to accommodate him. I was beginning to see signs of his excessive ego. Things would get much worse before it was all over.

Karen Brinette–1980 Sprayberry High
School Echo, Junior Year.

Travis Tritt–1980 Sprayberry High School
Echo, Junior Year.

Karen,
There is not much room here so I am going to be as brief as possible. I thank you for making this birthday the best I have ever had. You give me more joy and happiness than I ever thought I would have. You are my number one girl and I love you so much. I never thought I would fall in love, but you changed all that! You are very ~~important~~ important to my day to day life. I ~~know~~ know that you love me. Don't ~~ever~~ let that change.
Love always, Travis

This is what Travis wrote in my high-school yearbook.

59

Travis taking it easy between songs at an early show.

Travis and I at the Circle C Ranch in Alphoretta, Georgia. He is playing in a band called Southern Bred which played mainly in the Bible Belt.

Looking ten foot tall and bulletproof, Travis smiles for the camera prior to the prom.

I thought I could trust him with my heart.

Travis helped me hold on as we posed before my senior prom.

Prior to the senior prom, he loved me, but it was all about to change.

The kiss.

Travis accepting his high school diploma.

High School Graduation, 6-6-1980, Cobb County Civic Center.
My twin brother, Kevin, is standing behind me, to my left, in black.

Already a member of the Country Club, Travis serenades me at my home in the summer of 1981.

I could tell, even back then, that he was gonna be somebody, even though he did hit some t-r-o-u-b-l-e along the way.

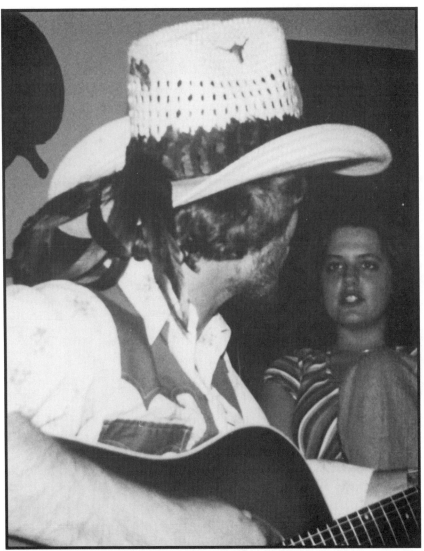

When Travis sang to me I wanted to drift off to dream in his arms.

Binette-Tritt

Rodney Binette and Jacqueline Binette of Marietta announce the engagement of their daughter, Karen Michelle, to James Travis Tritt, son of Mr. and Mrs. James Tritt of Marietta. The bride-elect is the grand-daughter of Mr. and Mrs. V.E. Cochran of Alpharetta and the late Mr. and Mrs. Alfred M. Binette. She is a graduate of Sprayberry High School and is employed by Dr. R.V. Caputo of Dunwoody. The future groom is the grandson of the Rev. and Mrs. J.T. Merritt of Ellijay and Nona Tritt of Marietta and the late Will Tritt. He is a graduate of Sprayberry High School and is employed by Dealer Supply Company in Marietta. The wedding is planned for 7 p.m. Sept. 25 at the Marietta First Assembly of God.

Photo: Norm Paschal Photography

We were so happy as we posed for our engagement picture that sometimes I find it hard to believe he doesn't love me anymore.

This is the car I rode in to the church on my wedding day.

My father and I on my wedding day.

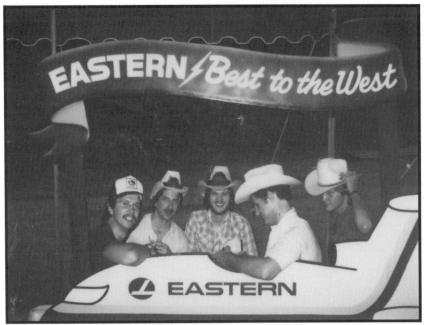

Prior to gig at Stone Mountain. The Lord had mercy on this working man.

With my pride and joy, Casey. I don't know what I would do without him.

Chapter Eleven

We returned home from our honeymoon to our little one-bedroom apartment, ready to get down to the business of being married. We were so thrilled to have a place to call ours, even if it was poorly decorated with hand-me-down furniture. We had the velour sofa from his mom's old house, as well as a matching orange velour stuffed chair with ottoman. We had his double bed from his childhood, and no other furniture in the bedroom. We couldn't afford a dresser or chest of drawers, so all of our clothes went into the closet on shelves and hangers. We had the table that he had refinished for me in the breakfast nook, and a small cast-off TV in the den. Between us, we were bringing home less than $300 per week. Our apartment rent was almost $400 a month, and with the truck payment, food, and utilities, things were going to be tight. We didn't care. We were finally married, and we knew we would probably have to eat hotddogs every day for a few months in order to get on our feet. Such is the way when you marry at nineteen years of age.

I've often wondered if the financial pressure that we were under was the cause of Travis's complete and utter lack of interest in sex after we were married. Almost all physical acts of love were completely stopped once we said I do. I've heard psychologists say that this can be due to many factors. The pressures of marriage sink in and can cause a glitch in the sex drive of a man. Sometimes, the man gets confused. He sees his wife take on all of the duties that his mother had previously performed, the wife becomes the caretaker instead of the mother, and the man can't perform sexually with her because she subconsciously reminds him of his mother. I never knew the reason behind Travis's lack of interest, but I can tell you that it quickly became a big sore spot in our marriage. I kept thinking that I was the problem, and it would take me years to realize that it was Travis all along, never me. His lack of interest hurt me terribly. It made me feel ugly and worthless. I had been raised to believe that after you marry, you and your husband are spiritually free to connect with each other in a physical sense. I felt that God wanted us to be close and to be able to enjoy each other the way that He had intended. It was as though sex was more appealing to Travis when it was forbidden. The moment that making love became morally acceptable, he lost interest. I tried to deal with the situation in many different ways, hoping to stumble upon the approach that would help both of us to understand where the problem lie. First, I tried being reasonable about it. I pointed out that it was now okay for us to act upon our desires. Then, I tried getting angry and confrontational. I told Travis that it wasn't fair for him to deny me my marital rights. Sex is supposed to play a large role in a healthy marriage. I told him that he was distancing me by keeping his body, and therefore his emotions, separate from me. Finally, I tried to ignore it, but it was difficult because it was such an obvious omission in our relationship. I eventually felt that if I pretended that there wasn't a problem it would somehow resolve itself. I knew that we would never get the difficulty resolved without professional help when Travis made a particularly hurtful comment to me during one of our discussions. I was trying to get him to open up and talk about his feelings, which I soon found was like pulling teeth.

"Why?" I lamented. "Please help me understand. Is it me? Is there something I've done? Tell me what I can do to fix this!"

"There is nothing that you can do," he replied sadly. "It's me, not you." He went on to say that I was a wonderful wife, and that he couldn't ask for a better wife. After a two-month dry spell, Travis approached me one night after we had gone to bed. He was feeling amorous and wanted to make love. After I recovered from my shock and surprise, we had a very tender exchange that brought tears to my eyes. It was as though he was trying to convey with his body alone that he did love me and that he wanted to have romantic feelings towards me again. It was as though he knew that the feelings had disappeared for him and he was trying to find them again. I was very touched. (He did something after that incident that was very indicative of the type of person that he was. He asked me if I was thirsty. After I said yes, he said that he would go and fix me a glass of orange juice. I thought that was sweet, since he rarely offered to do those kinds of things for me.) He had, in fact, told me once that I was put on this earth to serve him and to meet all of his needs. I was too immature to ask him about *my* needs. Besides, I was happy if Travis was happy, period. He left the room, and I closed my eyes to ponder this man whom I loved so much. After about 20 minutes, wondering what was keeping him, I went to the doorway of the bedroom where I could see into the kitchen. The orange juice was the concentrated kind that you keep in the freezer and mix with water when you are ready to serve it. Instead of mixing it in a plastic pitcher, he had gotten out a blender that we had received as a wedding present. After making the juice, he proceeded to take the entire blender apart and wash and dry each and every piece by hand before reassembling the blender and putting it away. I teased him for months about his "one-hour glass of orange juice." That was one of the happier times of our life in that apartment. We started calling each other by silly little pet names... he was "Mister Man" and I was "Mrs. Man." I don't know how we came up with those, but we used those names more frequently than our given ones.

It was during this time that Travis and I were asked to be models in a fashion show. Travis bought all of his clothes from a big country-western store in Marietta called "Horsetown." We were there one afternoon purchasing a couple of pairs of Levi's for him when the owner of the store approached us. He told us that Horsetown was doing a fashion show at Miss Kitty's, a large country bar, in Marietta, and he needed people to model the clothes. Since our friends were also participating, we agreed. The owner gave me several dresses to model, one of which I absolutely loved. It was navy and white with a square neckline, puffed sleeves, and a full skirt. We had a great time doing the show and returned all of the clothing afterwards. The next day when I got home from work, there was a big white box with a red bow on the kitchen table. Upon opening it, I discovered the navy and white dress. Unbeknownst to me, Travis had purchased the dress the night before because he knew how much I loved it. It was one of the nicest things he had ever done for me. I wasn't totally shocked, because he could be so kind and generous at times.

We continued to work at our respective jobs and celebrated with Mark and Kathie at the arrival of their son, Luke. Band practice was put on hold for a while. They still lived with Mark's parents and they needed some time with the baby. Also, we thought the noise level in the house during rehearsals would be too much for an infant. But shortly after the birth of their son, Mark and Kathie moved into an apartment just down the road from us. Practice would resume every Wednesday night. Most of the time, I would stay with Kathie and the baby while Travis went to rehearsals. Kathie and I had developed a good friendship. We used to talk about the boys that we were married to and how difficult marriage could be sometimes. There was one particular problem that I was facing and I couldn't talk to anyone about it, not even Kathie: Travis absolutely refused to allow me to have anything to do with my mother. After I got married, she started dating a handsome man named Larry who was a wonderful companion to her. He also happened to be her junior by sixteen years. They soon moved in together and began what would be a long, happy relationship. Travis absolutely could not deal with it. He said that her behavior was shameful, and that as long as she continued I wasn't to see her or speak to her. Needless to say, I did what I was told. I can't even begin to describe how much this hurt my mom. I broke off all contact with her coldly and abruptly. Travis had convinced me that my mom was a bad influence and that she would probably try to break up my marriage if given half a chance—a chance I wasn't about to give her.

Chapter Twelve

Christmas of 1982 arrived. Travis and I were making preparations for what would be our only Christmas celebration in the apartment. We purchased a small tree and a few ornaments. As poor as we were, we managed to get each other nice gifts. It was what I called a "clothing Christmas." I got him about twelve cowboy shirts, and he got me dresses. I guess he was tired of seeing me in jeans all the time. The dresses were a style I usually shied away from: long-sleeved, high-necked country dresses trimmed in lace with flowered prints. I didn't much care for them, but I wore them to make him happy. That was also the year that we bought matching split leather fringed jackets. His was a dark buckskin, while mine was a lighter doeskin. We thought we looked pretty cute. I guess this was the beginning of the obsession that Travis now seems to have with fringed jackets. It was around this time that I saw yet another example of Travis's excessive temper. The truck had been involved in a wreck. Travis wasn't at fault, but the left front corner of the truck body had to be replaced. Travis had to live without his precious vehicle for about two weeks, and he was getting irritable. Finally, it was returned to him completely repaired and freshly painted. We were coming home from dinner at his parents' house, and after stopping to get a Sunday paper at a convenience store, he parked in front of our building right next to a curb. The curb was on his side, and since he'd parked very close to another car on my side, I decided to slide across the front seat and get out on his side. That way, I figured, I wouldn't risk hitting the other car with the newly painted passenger door. I stepped down from the truck with the bulky newspaper in my arms. The grass was wet and I had on high heels, so I decided to walk along the curb to the front of the truck. Big mistake. I lost my balance and fell against the new paint. I didn't do any harm to it, but Travis went bananas! He started yelling at me in the parking lot. "How can you be so stupid?" he screamed at the top of his lungs. "Get in the house... NOW! I can't believe you would do something like that!"

I immediately started trying to placate him. "Honey, it was an accident. I didn't do it on purpose. I really don't think I hurt the truck. I just fell against it." Travis wouldn't listen to reason and he continued to rail at me once we got inside the apartment. I was crushed and bewildered at his behavior. He didn't even once ask me if I was all right. His only concern was for his truck. This was the second time in our relationship that he had put his concern for the truck before his concern for me. How could he love me as much as he claimed and yet treat me this way? Was my well-being less important to him than his vehicle? I simply could not understand his priorities. When he was through yelling at me, he began to ignore me. He wouldn't speak to me when I asked him a question, and he spent the night on the sofa. I went to bed in tears. Finally, around 4:00 A.M., I couldn't bear it any longer. I got up and went into the den. He was awake as well, and I begged him to forgive me and come to bed. Even if I had done nothing wrong, Travis had a way of turning things around so that I was apologizing to him for something that he had done to me. He finally did forgive me for falling against his cherished pickup truck and joined me in the double bed. The next morning, he acted as if nothing had happened. The blinders that I had been wearing due to my intense love for him were slowly coming off, and I didn't particularly like what I was seeing.

After the holidays, I changed jobs again and Travis and I moved into his mother's old house. I was not happy with my job at the doctor's office. A new office manager had been hired, and he and I had extreme personality differences. I quit the job before I had a new one. I was unemployed for about eight weeks, and we moved during that time. Gwen offered to rent the house to us for $250 a month. Since we were down to one income, we gratefully accepted. This would also give us a place for the band to practice without having to further impose on Mark's parents. We moved in at the end of January 1983. I was very happy about having a house as opposed to an apartment. It was a three-bedroom, traditional brick and wood L-shaped house with a two car garage. It had been built in the 1970s, and the decor reflected the style of that era. It had greenish-yellow, long pile shag carpet with avocado green kitchen appliances and countertops.

Though the house was a few years out of date, I thought it was charming.

We quickly set up housekeeping under Gwen's watchful eye. The house was a investment to her, and she wanted to make sure that we took good care of it. She made sure that I knew not to use Comet cleanser in the stainless steel kitchen sink, and she quickly extracted a promise from Travis to take good care of the lawn. I must say that at the time I resented Gwen's concerns regarding our ability to take care of a house, but now that I have a child of my own, I can better understand her position. Band practice resumed the first week that we were in the house. It was during this time that we met Jimmy. I don't know where he came from—he just showed up on our front doorstep one Wednesday night. He was a friend of someone's, and he had come over to play his guitar with the guys. He had an excellent voice and while he couldn't play lead, he could play rhythm, and he was exactly what the band needed. The guys asked Jimmy if he would like to join the band. He readily agreed and the new Southern Bred was formed. Jimmy and I developed an unusual relationship. Travis and I were continuing to have our share of problems and he was still having difficulty in the bedroom. I eventually found out from Jimmy that he and his wife were having similar problems, but the tables were turned. Jimmy was in my position, married to someone who had problems demonstrating physical affection. Jimmy and I had become rather close friends and because Travis wouldn't talk to me about it, I turned to Jimmy for advice. After fighting with Travis, I would call Jimmy to get his opinion on how I should handle a particular circumstance. I assumed that it would help me to get another male's opinion of the situation. Jimmy was very understanding of my plight and it never seemed to be an imposition to him when I called for advice. He once suggested that I try and seduce Travis. At Jimmy's prompting, I purchased a sexy black negligee and decided to surprise my husband. One night before Travis arrived home from work, I put on my new nightgown, built a fire in the fireplace in the den, and brought down all of our pillows and blankets from the bed. I placed a bottle of champagne in the ice bucket and settled down to wait. My heart started thumping loudly in my ears when I heard the truck pull into the garage. I was scared to death! I wanted so much for this to work, but at the same time I was terrified of rejection. As I heard him walk up the basement stairs, I struck a sexy pose in front of the fire. Travis walked into the room and just stood there staring at me. I didn't say anything to him... I just smiled shyly and held out my hand. He turned and left the room without saying a word. He walked upstairs and I heard the bedroom door slam shut. I was devastated! I felt so humiliated and ugly. I know that I sat there and cried for hours while the fire died, as did a great deal of the love and respect I had felt for Travis. His actions were slowly chipping away at my love for him, and I wondered how soon it would be before there was nothing left.

Chapter Thirteen

The next day, nothing was said about the night before. My eyes were red and swollen from crying so much, but Travis never mentioned it. While I was downstairs wallowing in self-pity and feeling generally worthless, he had been upstairs playing his guitar, as was his usual pattern. He played his guitar for several hours every day. What at first had been a romantic attraction had become a constant thorn in my side. I felt that he loved his music more than me, and I was suffering from the lack of attention. I remember lamenting to Jimmy once that Travis would love me more if I had a long neck and six strings. I didn't expect him to put me before his music, but I at least wanted to be as important. I guess that's what people mean when they say that it takes a special person to be married to a musician. I decided that being unemployed was adding to my sense of low self-esteem, so I began to search for a job. I didn't want to go back to work in the medical field, so I scanned the classified ads for something new and different. I finally accepted a job offer as a receptionist at one of Atlanta's top-rated hair salons. This job would prove to be very detrimental to my marriage. I had a very outdated appearance and the salon wanted me to look fashionable and modern. They cut my long hair to my shoulders and gave me a perm. I couldn't wear country clothes to work, so I purchased a new wardrobe in the latest fashion trends. Bright, bold, colors were in style and mini-skirts were making a comeback. On my first day, Travis left for work about an hour and a half before I was due at the salon. After preparing his usual breakfast of eggs, sausage, and homemade biscuits, I kissed him good-bye and hurried to get ready for work. When I arrived at the salon, the hairdressers fixed my hair and put styling gel in it to give it the popular "wet" look. One of the hairdressers re-applied my make-up and put a brightly-colored lipstick on me while I stared dubiously into the mirror. They were in the image-building business and I definitely needed to look sleek and sophisticated for my new position, as I was the first person that the customers came into contact with upon entering the salon. "What's wrong?" she asked. "I don't know about this," I replied. "My husband doesn't let me wear lipstick. He really doesn't like a lot of make-up either. I don't think he's going to like me looking like this."

I was correct in my assumption. When I arrived home, Travis took one look at my face, my hair, and my outfit and exploded! We were going out that night and I was going to go without changing. Travis had other ideas. "Get in the bathroom and wash that grease out of your hair and wipe that crap off your face while you're at it!" he yelled when he saw me. "I'm not going anywhere with a wife who looks like she has greasy hair and who is dressed like a slut!" I started apologizing and tried to explain to him that I needed to change my appearance in order to fit in at work. He just ignored me, and I finally gave up trying to make him understand. I had liked the way that my co-workers had made me look... kind of sexy and up-to-date. Travis preferred me the old way... unadorned and natural.

The new band started playing at little country-and-western dives around town. Even though I had to dress in the latest styles for work, at home and at gigs I dressed in jeans and boots to please my husband. Southern Bred became fairly popular and soon had a small following. I never missed a performance. I would sit in the bars at a little table, drinking beer and listening to all of the songs that I now knew by heart. I would sing harmony under my breath and patiently wait until break time. Travis always dedicated at least one or two songs to me every night. I particularly remember "You were Always on My Mind" by Willie Nelson and "The Wind Beneath My Wings," as well as "Close Enough to Perfect" by Alabama. I loved hearing him say "This next one is for my wife," then watching the women in the audience try to figure out who his wife was. I was always so proud when he came straight to my table during breaks and I saw the jealous looks that were pointed in my direction. I wished things could be as good at home as they seemed to be in public. I felt as though I was growing, both professionally and personally, and it seemed to me that Travis resented the new changes in my life. We began having enormous fights over absurd things.

One night when I was making spaghetti for dinner I was scrambling the ground beef in a skillet over high heat. I asked Travis to watch the meat for me while I got the garlic out of the refrigerator. When I returned to the stove, I noticed that he had turned the burner down. I turned the burner back up and continued making dinner. He came back into the kitchen and again turned the burner to low, stating that his mother had taught him to always cook hamburger meat that way. I readjusted the knob and told him that my mother had told *me* otherwise. I never should have brought up my mother, because it just enraged him and we got into a heated argument over something as trivial as the correct way to cook ground beef! I was too young to understand the meaning of a power struggle. Other instances began surfacing which confirmed my suspicions that our relationship was deteriorating.

I had grilled pork chops for dinner. Everything was ready, including the vegetables that had come out of our garden. Travis had heard the call of the trowel and had decided that he would plant an extensive garde—and that even though I had no clue as to how it was done, I would freeze and can the fruits (or vegetables) of his labor. Dinner was on the table and he was out front doing yard work. I called out the window for him to come in and sat down to wait. Five, ten, fifteen minutes went by, and no sign of Travis. I was getting irritated. I'm still this way, even today—if I go to all of the trouble of putting a nice meal on the table, you had better be considerate enough to eat it when I tell you it's ready. I went to the window again and through tightly clenched teeth asked him to please come inside, when what I really wanted to do was to throw the now-cold food out onto the lawn with him. He said he'd be right in. After a few more minutes, I was really mad. In a rare display of anger, I threw open the front door and yelled at him to come in the house immediately. He yelled back and said that he'd come in "when he was good and damn ready!" I showed him my temper for the very first time in two and a half years.

"Well, you can just go to hell!" I slammed the front door shut and stalked upstairs to fume. He came running in after me and told me that I had better not ever embarrass him like that again! I had yelled loud enough for the neighbors to hear, and he didn't want them to think that he was a wimp because he allowed his wife to talk to him that way. I had calmed down by that time and I quietly tried to explain my position, but yet again my words fell on deaf ears. I went downstairs, threw the dinner into the trash, and went upstairs to cry. Travis got out his guitar and played for the rest of the night.

One night I decided to try my hand at making good old Southern fried chicken. I vaguely remembered how my mom had made it, soaking the chicken for hours in buttermilk before double-coating it in flour. I thought that Travis would enjoy it, so I set out to create the best fried chicken in the history of the South! My efforts proved worthwhile, and while it wasn't as tasty as Mom's, I thought it was good. After I brought Travis his plate in the living room, I got my plate and sat down with him to enjoy my meal. After a few bites I said "Well... do you like it?"

"Yeah," he replied with his mouth full. "It's okay... but I wouldn't serve it to company." So much for pleasing my husband. That comment really hurt me. I had tried to do something right, and I had failed again. Travis continued to belittle my efforts to please him. He had an annoying habit of shaking his empty glass at me when he wanted a refill on his drink. Without so much as a glance or a word in my direction, he would extend his glass towards me and rattle the ice. That was my cue to get up and get him more iced tea or whatever he was drinking. I was usually exhausted from work, but I always did it, when I should have said "Your legs aren't broken—if you're thirsty, you get it yourself," but I never did. (In September of 1989, after "Country Club" had become a big hit, Travis was playing at Miss Kitty's in Underground Atlanta. Underground Atlanta is a large shopping and entertainment complex in the heart of downtown. I was moonlighting as a waitress there. I ran into Travis in the office behind the stage. After exchanging a few pleasantries, I asked him if he wanted something to drink. He said yes and I brought him a Coke. When I handed it to him, I shuddered and said, "Oh, I don't like this feeling. It reminds me of the old days." He just laughed and said, "Yeah, the old days were pretty good, weren't they?" I thought to myself, "Maybe from your perspective, but then again, YOU weren't the one being stalked by a madman with a gun!")

Chapter Fourteen

Our power struggles continued into the summer of 1983. I was still working full-time at the salon, and trying harder than ever to make Travis happy. There were no outward signs of the emotional turmoil that I was suffering, but I knew inside that I was not the same woman that he'd married. I was growing up. I wanted to succeed in my career and be a loving and supportive wife, but something had to give. I knew deep in my heart that I would have to be the one doing all the giving. Travis decided to open a checking account with a local bank without informing me. Prior to this, we had been paying our bills either in cash or by money order. It made sense to get a checking account, although I never understood why he never told me about it beforehand. The mail had been delivered that Saturday afternoon. I noticed a small brown box from a bank, opened it, and discovered that not only had Travis opened an account, he had neglected to put my name on the checks. When I later questioned him about it, he told me that it was "no big deal"—that I was to give him my paychecks and he would give me a weekly allowance of ten dollars. At the time I thought this was unfair as I was earning just as much as he was. He said that he wanted to be in charge of our finances. I was willing to accept this latest decision of his until he made his last comment on the subject. He just laughed, patted me on the arm, and said, "Honey, you know that you're not bright enough to be able to handle a checking account."

Tears of humiliation streamed down my face as I said, "What are you talking about? I handle all of the paperwork for the salon, including taxes and payroll! You actually think that I can't cope with one tiny little CHECKBOOK?" He just continued to laugh as he walked upstairs to get ready for rehearsal. I stayed downstairs, fuming, until the doorbell rang. While he was letting the band in, I went upstairs and didn't come down for the rest of the night. I eventually recovered from this latest bruise to my ego, and I also started turning over my paychecks to Travis. We were fighting almost every day, and I was trying to make peace with him. I guess it was my way of bailing water out of a sinking ship. Travis was pulling away from me and I could feel it. I was so frightened. I tightened my emotional hold on him in a desperate attempt to salvage what little remained of our relationship. I worshiped this man. My marital vows were more sacred to me at this point than they had been during the entire duration of our marriage. I had no one to turn to. At the salon, my co-workers began to notice my changing personality. Where I was once carefree and bubbly, I was now solemn and depressed. My eyes would well up with tears if anyone asked me a question regarding my husband. I was so scared. I needed help. One night, shortly after the checking account incident, Travis was going over to a friend's house to play poker. It was a "no girls allowed" get-together, and I was heartsick at the thought of an entire evening without him. I moped around the house with a dismal look on my face while Travis was getting ready to go. At around 7:00 p.m., I went upstairs and put on my nightgown. Even though it was still daylight outside, I brushed my teeth and crawled into bed in a full-blown depression. When Travis came out of the bathroom, and saw me lying in bed he said, "What are you doing? It's only 7:00. Why are you in bed?"

"Because there's nothing to do when you're not here," I answered pitifully. "I might as well go to sleep, and when I wake up tomorrow, you'll be back." Travis just threw up his hands and said in disgust, "God, get some friends, get a life, get something! You're too dependent on me. I can't be everything to you!"

"But I don't want to do anything if I can't do it with you," I replied. He turned around and left as I started crying. The phone rang sometime around 4:00 A.M. It was Travis. He had wrecked the truck and he wanted me to come and get him. After making sure that he wasn't injured, I asked him how the accident had occurred. He told me that it was incredibly foggy outside. He couldn't see where he was going, and he had crossed a two lane road and hit a large oak tree. I remember saying to him, "It's so foggy that YOU can't see to drive, and yet you want ME to come and get you?"

Needless to say, I got dressed and drove through fog that was so thick I could barely see two feet in front of me, and picked up my tired and cranky husband. We seemed to call a truce after that incident. We started getting along better and I was happy because Travis was being nicer to me. Christmas of 1983 was approaching and, like everyone else, he was striving to be more understanding during the holiday season. I was making preparations for the Christmas Eve dinner that I was going to serve my immediate family—everyone except my mother. Though it had been over a year since I had had any contact with her, she still continued to try to reach me by sending birthday and Christmas presents along with cards. I was secretly pleased at her attempts. It made me feel loved to know that even though I had banished her from my life, Mom continued to reach out to me. I always hid these gifts from Travis. We were having enough trouble as it was. My father and his fiance, as well as Keith and my new sister-in-law Renee, were scheduled to arrive soon. My brother Kevin was also there. Though it was not yet Christmas morning, Travis had already given me my present... a brand new expensive bedroom suite complete with king-sized bed. It had been delivered the 23rd of December, and even though I knew of the gift in advance, I was thrilled! Maybe the new bed would see more action than the old one had! We had been sleeping on the double bed from his childhood and we still kept our clothes on shelves in the closet, just as we had done in the apartment. My new bedroom was beautiful, and I thanked Travis repeatedly for his thoughtfulness. When my family arrived bearing gifts, we piled them under the Christmas tree to open later. We adjourned to the dining room and enjoyed a traditional meal of turkey and dressing and all the trimmings. Later, when it was time to unwrap presents, my father laid a large box on my lap and made everyone watch while I opened it. Inside was a gorgeous fur coat! I jumped up and ran to my dad and gave him a big hug. It was unusual for my father to be that extravagant with a gift, and I knew it. He wanted so much for me to be pleased with the coat, so I continued to rave over it for the remainder of the evening. I was so caught up in the festivities that I didn't even notice Travis' darkening mood. Soon, it was time for my family to leave. I walked them to the door, gave everyone a hug and kiss, and thanked my dad again for the beautiful coat. I shut the door and walked back into the living room to clean up. Travis was sitting in the armchair, just staring at me with a look of utter contempt on his face. When I asked him what was wrong, he jumped up and began yelling at me that I had liked my dad's gift more than his. I told him that he was crazy and I tried to explain to him why the coat had meant so much to me, but he wouldn't listen. He kept insisting that I would rather have had a coat than a new bedroom. I had come to realize that I couldn't reason with Travis when his ego was involved. I shook my head, cleaned up the mess, and went to bed. He slept on the sofa on Christmas Eve of 1983. Christmas Day arrived and I felt us slipping into the old routine. New Year's Eve was just as lonely for me as Christmas Eve had been. No pizza... no champagne. Travis slept on the couch that night as I cried myself to sleep in the new, empty, king-sized bed. I should have known then that the painful loneliness of that night was an indication of the year ahead.

Chapter Fifteen

Our marriage was deteriorating rapidly. I started talking to Travis about getting a puppy. Some women, when their relationships begin to become unraveled, think that a baby will be the glue that holds everything together. I knew that I was too immature at twenty years of age to become a mother. A dog seemed to be the next best solution. After some coaxing and cajoling Travis reluctantly agreed, and we made a trip to the Cobb County Humane Society. I didn't want to just *buy* a puppy... I wanted to *rescue* one. Travis asked me if I had a particular breed in mind. I told him, "No, I'll know which one I'm supposed to have when we get there." There were at least twenty or thirty puppies inside. Sitting forlornly in the corner was a little long-haired female with the saddest brown eyes. I asked the attendant if I could hold her, and that was all that it took. She stole my heart! I looked at Travis pleadingly and said, "I want this one... can I have her?" He grudgingly said yes, and we signed the adoption papers and took her from one troubled home to another. Due to her pretty golden color, I named her "Honey". I eventually discovered that Honey was part golden retriever and part cocker spaniel. On her first night with us, we put her in a box in the kitchen with a blanket and a small clock. I had read that the ticking of a clock can soothe a distressed animal. The clock reminds them of their mother's heartbeat. Travis wanted to put her in the dog house in our backyard. I put my foot down and said that she had to be inside because it was January and only twenty degrees outside. If Honey was sleeping outside, so was I! I had become very attached to her in the few hours that she had been with me. I could feel myself pouring out to her all of the love and affection that I so desperately needed to give. She returned my affection by wanting to stay glued to my lap and by happily licking my face each time she got the chance. I loved smelling her little "puppy-breath" smell. After assuring her that I wasn't going to be far away, Travis and I went to bed. We could hear her crying all the way upstairs. I wanted to go and get her and bring her into the bed with us, but Travis absolutely would not allow it. I stayed awake long after he had fallen asleep, then crept quietly downstairs to hold and comfort my dog. Travis found me in the kitchen the next morning, sitting on the floor, propped up against the wall. Honey and I were fast asleep. The puppy was a welcome diversion for me and she made me very happy, except for one small problem... she wouldn't eat. By the second day, I still couldn't get her to touch a bite of food. I had contacted the Humane Society and had followed their suggestions for persuading Honey to eat. I purchased tempting dog treats at the grocery store, and even bought her some liver-flavored canned cat food to stimulate her appetite. She simply would not eat. By the third day, I was really getting worried. She had lost some weight and her rib cage was beginning to show. I was holding her in the armchair and crying when Travis came home from work that day. "Travis," I said through my tears, "she still hasn't eaten anything. I'm afraid that she is going to die. What should we do?"

"I think we should take her back and get another one," he replied coldly. "There is obviously something wrong with her. Besides, I got you a dog so that you would be happy. Now all you do is sit around and cry over it."

I couldn't believe he'd actually suggested that we return Honey. She was a part of our family. When I made this comment to Travis, he said, "You have to take her back tomorrow morning. We'll go get another one this weekend." That was it. I was losing my dog because my husband didn't have enough compassion in his heart to work through her problem. I thought that I knew just how she felt. I got up the next morning, called the Humane Society, and told them that my husband was forcing me to give Honey back to them. They told me to drive her to a house that was fairly close to mine. An elderly couple lived there, and they frequently took animals into their home until suitable owners could be found. I nearly wrecked the car several times during the short drive to the house. I was crying so hard and trying to hold Honey and steer the car at the same time. When I arrived, the elderly man was waiting for me on the front porch. Apparently, he'd received a phone call and was expecting us. I slowly walked up to the house and handed him my dog without a word. I ran back to my car and watched him carry her into the house. My heart actually hurt, I was grieving so. Travis was by now a master at manipulating me. He would do something that would bring me joy, and then somehow find a way to tear that joy away from me. I loved this helpless little animal and I cried for the rest of that week, but Travis seemed oblivious to my pain. Returning Honey was the hardest thing that I'd ever had to do. That weekend, we drove to the animal shelter once again to choose another pet. I was extremely disinterested in the puppies that they had in the pens that day. Travis, on the other hand, was very enthusiastic, and promptly selected a little tan and black short-haired female. She had a little red bandana tied around her neck and she was very energetic. We signed the papers for this dog, and put her in the truck to go home. I ignored the puppy and sat as far away from her as I could and just stared out of the window in silence. Suddenly, I felt a little, cold, wet nose on my hand. I looked down to see her staring up at me with these big, playful brown eyes. My heart softened a bit, and I relented enough to let her crawl into my lap. Travis noticed all of this without saying a word. We decided to name her "Sandy." She was part German Shepherd and part retriever. I never felt the same way about Sandy as I had felt about Honey. Travis thought she was the perfect dog for us until she too refused to eat. We were at our wits' end with the puppy situation. After calling the shelter yet again, a woman there stated that sometimes puppies need the competition of another animal in order to want to eat. She suggested that we keep Sandy and get another dog; that way, she would be encouraged to feed herself. She told us to drive to the home of the elderly couple where I had left Honey. They had a litter of husky/shepherd mixes that were ready to leave their mother. We went to the house that night to look at the puppies. When we arrived, the couple led us around the back of the house to a dog pen filled with puppies. It was fairly dark and it was difficult to distinguish one puppy from the next. Suddenly, a familiar bark came from inside the pen. My heart soared! Honey was still there! I thought that she had been sent to a new home. It had never crossed my mind that she might still be there. I called her name, and she came running up to the gate and poked her little nose through the chain-link fence. I knelt down and stroked her, saying her name over and over. I looked up at Travis and begged him to let me have her again. I told him that she would probably eat since we now had Sandy. They could help each other with their problem. Without a moment's hesitation, he readily agreed. I was emotionally spent after we left that house. First Travis gave me the puppy, then he devastated me by taking her away, then he gave her to me again. I felt as though my heart had been ripped apart and sewn back together several times. We took her home that very night, and each of them devoured a big bowl of puppy food. It worked! Now we each had a dog... Honey was mine and Sandy was his. I was ecstatic to have her home again. That February, it warmed up a little outside and Travis decided that it was time for them to be outside permanently. Nothing I could say would change his mind about this. I couldn't stand for them to be outside in the cold, but Travis was adamant. Valentine's Day arrived. Because of the dissension in our marriage, I didn't really expect a gift. Travis had ridden to work that day on a motorcycle that he had recently purchased from his father. I hated it with a passion! Travis always wanted me to ride it with him, regardless of the fact that I felt very unsafe when I was on it. I was unsure of Travis' skill level when it came to riding a motorcycle. When I heard him pull into the driveway, I started putting dinner on the table. He walked into the kitchen and handed me a new curling iron, stating that it was the only gift he could find that would fit on the back of the Harley. I needed a new curling iron and I was happy that he had at least gotten me something that I could use. Two months later, almost to the day, Travis walked through the front door and stunned me by delivering the news that would shatter my world.

Chapter Sixteen

Spring arrived early. I was more than ready. April of 1984 was warm and sunny. The puppies were getting bigger and more playful. Our relationship, at least in my heart, seemed to be improving. Our sex life was still non-existent, but I felt that there was hope for improvement once we resolved our problems. Many nights, after cooking our dinner on the grill, Travis and I would take Sandy and Honey into the front yard to play with us while we were doing yard work. One night, the four of us were romping in the yard. Travis and I were tossing a frisbee, and the puppies chased it while it flew through the air. They became exhausted running back and forth on the lawn between us. After about an hour, we flopped down on the grass to rest and watch the magnificent Georgia sunset. Travis was propped up against a tree in the yard, and I had my head on his lap. The dogs had fallen asleep while lying next to us. I looked up at my husband and shyly told him that I was going to go in and take a bubble bath. I asked him if he would like to accompany me. He looked at me dubiously and I told him that I wasn't trying to seduce him. He agreed to join me, as long as I understood that he was in no mood to make love. I agreed and after putting the animals up for the night, we went upstairs. When we were through with our bath, we lay in bed and talked. It had been a long time since we'd had a serious discussion about our relationship. I reminded him of a comment that he had made to me before we'd ever married. Travis told me that if things ever became bad between us, we would go to see a marriage counselor. He remembered making that statement and decided that the time had arrived for us to seek professional help. I told him that my parents had a good friend who was a psychiatrist and marriage counselor. I thought that he would be fairly inexpensive, due to the doctor's relationship with my parents. He had counseled them for a period of time before they separated. Although he was unsuccessful in helping them to sustain their marriage, he was able to help them work through some personal problems. Travis agreed to meet with him and told me to schedule an appointment. The next couple of days were peaceful ones in our home. I was relieved that Travis was willing to see a therapist. Our financial situation was a little tight, and it made me feel good that he was willing to budget our household expenses in such a way that we could afford the services of a marriage counselor. During this time, I contacted my mother for the first time in a year and a half. Something inside of me must have sensed the disaster that was looming, because I felt the sudden urge to talk to my mom. I called her at work and we spoke guardedly on the phone for a few minutes. She asked me to meet her for lunch, and I agreed. I did not tell Travis of my intentions, because we were having enough problems as it was. When I met Mom that Saturday, she gave me a big hug and told me how much she had missed me. I admitted that I'd missed her as well. She asked me how things were going in my marriage and I lied through my teeth. I told her that everything was wonderful, and that we were even thinking of starting a family. It couldn't have been further from the truth, but I didn't want her to know how bad things really were. She told me years later that she suspected that things were not as they seemed, but she didn't want to be an interfering mother. We left the restaurant with tentative plans to talk again soon. A few days later, on April 12, 1984, I was sitting in in the living room in my nightgown reading a book. Travis was at his parents' house picking up something for the motorcycle. He had been gone for about two hours, and I was beginning to worry. When he came in around 8:30, he was in a foul mood. He came into the living room and with no forewarning said, "I've decided not to see a marriage counselor, especially not the one that your parents went to. He'd probably take your side, since he knows your family, and I'm not going to sit there and let him blame me for all of our problems!"

I tried to reason with him and tell him that I was sure that this would not happen, but Travis refused to cooperate. I even offered to locate another marriage counselor and told him that it didn't really matter who we saw as long as we saw someone. Travis just shook his head and stated flatly, "No, I don't want to do that. I want a divorce."

I just stared at him in utter disbelief. I had no earthly idea that last statement was coming. "You *can't!*" I cried out. "Please don't tell me that you want a divorce! We'll work it out, I know we will. We just need some help. Oh God, Travis! Please, please don't give up on us!" After a few more minutes of emotional discussion, he decided that maybe what we really needed was some time apart. He suggested a trial separation and I readily agreed—anything to keep him from talking about divorce. Since we were living in his mother's house, Travis decided that he would stay and I would move back in with my father for a little while. He said that he would help me pack during the upcoming weekend, and we agreed on Sunday as the day that I would leave. I believed that if I tried harder, did more, loved more, it would work. I vowed to do everything in my power to keep him from divorcing me. The next day was a Wednesday, and since Travis had to get up early to go to work, he left me and went upstairs to bed. I stayed downstairs for hours, trying to decide how I was going to keep my marriage from completely falling apart. I finally fell asleep on the couch without coming to any resolutions. The sun shining through the front windows woke me up Wednesday morning. After making sure that Travis was awake and in the shower, I went into the kitchen and began to make him breakfast just as I had for the previous 563 days of our marriage. I was trying to behave as normally as possible, which I tend to do in the face of a disaster. I was reacting in my typical fashion, pretending that everything was perfectly fine. Travis didn't seem surprised when I handed him a brown paper bag with his breakfast sandwich inside. He kissed me on the cheek and told me to have a nice day at work, then left for his job at Dealer's Supply Company. I started to cry as I heard the truck pull out of the driveway, and I didn't stop for the next two days. I called my boss at the salon and told her that I wouldn't be able to work that day because of personal problems. She could tell that I was crying and asked me what was wrong, but I couldn't tell her. After I hung up the phone, I sat down on the kitchen floor and sobbed for at least an hour. My heart was breaking and I literally felt like I was going to die. I felt so alone, and I knew deep inside that no one was going to help me out of this mess. I was no longer my mother's little girl. She couldn't just kiss this and make the hurt go away. I no longer knew if she even wanted to. I remember feeling that my life was over. I felt that no one had ever been through this much pain and lived. This was my punishment for what? I had no answers. I needed to be comforted, but there was no person that I could turn to with this kind of problem. I did the next best thing. In an act of defiance against Travis, I let the dogs into the house. He never allowed them into the house, but I needed their love and affection so desperately at that moment, I didn't care what Travis' rules were. I even fed them the left-over steaks that were in the refrigerator from a couple of nights before. Travis refused to allow me to feed them table scraps and bought them the least expensive dog food that he could find. Sandy and Honey were ecstatic to finally be inside, and were equally thrilled with their breakfast. It made me feel better to do something nice for them... especially since I knew that Travis would be furious if he ever found out about it. I spent the rest of that day in tears. I can't remember what Travis said when he got home that night or exactly what happened, but I do remember very clearly what took place on the following day,

Thursday, April 14, 1984. That day ended with me running for my life.

Chapter Seventeen

I went to work the next morning. Thursday was usually a busy day at the hair salon, and they needed me. I arrived at the shop still crying from the events of the previous two days. I spent most of that morning sitting in the office. I managed to call Mark's wife Kathie to tell her that Travis and I were separating. She was very concerned about me and wanted to see me that night. She asked me if I wanted to meet for a drink after work. I said yes, since I didn't really want to be at home alone. Travis had told me that morning that he would be late getting home because he was going out with the guys after work. Apparently Kathie told Mark of our plans and Mark told Travis, because I got a phone call at work around 11:30 A.M. Travis was very angry at me for planning to go out with Kathie after work. He yelled at me over the phone, telling me "No wife of mine is going to sit at a bar and act like a slut! If you want to act single, then by God, you'll be single! I want you and your things out of my house by six o'clock tonight!" Then he hung up on me. I crumbled. I did the only thing that I could think of at that moment—I called my mother. When I told her what Travis had said, she didn't ask any questions. She simply stated that if I would give her directions to the house, she would meet me there and help me get my things. I hung up the phone, told my boss I was leaving for the day, and drove home. After I arrived, I went upstairs to pack a few of my clothes and personal items. I put everything in a small suitcase, placed it on the dining room table, and sat down to wait for my mom. She rang the doorbell about twenty minutes later. My jaw dropped when I opened the door. She was standing on the front step with both of my brothers and several girls who worked for her at the doctor's office. Parked in the driveway was a huge flatbed truck with side rails! I was very confused as I let them into the house. Mom asked me if I had everything I wanted, and I nodded and pointed to my suitcase. "Is that all you're taking?", she asked incredulously. "Yes", I replied through my tears. "Oh no, it's not," my mother replied firmly. She went outside and brought in a bunch of boxes from the truck. Mom went into the kitchen and began placing pots and pans and dishes into the boxes. "WHAT are you doing?" I asked her. "Travis told me to take my clothes and make-up and stuff. I can't take all of this—he didn't tell me to!"

Mom said, "I don't care what he told you. You are not leaving this house until you take everything that you are entitled to. You might not get another chance. You'd better take what you want now."

She went into the living room and picked up a knick-knack that was on the coffee table. "Do you want this?" she asked me.

"No," I replied.

"Yes, you do... you just don't know it," she said. She then walked over and pointed to a large picture that was hanging over the fireplace. "Do you want this?" she asked me again.

I said, "No, Mom."

"Well, I do," she replied as she took the picture down. I was following her around the house, watching as she gave orders to Kevin, Keith, and the girls who had come to help. We had made our way back into the living room when I said "Mom, you have to stop! I can't take all of this stuff! Travis will kill me! You don't understand, we have to put it back!"

My mother simply said, "Hush, Karen, and pick up your end of the couch!"

"NO!!", I cried out. "We absolutely cannot take the sofa! It belonged to his mother. He will absolutely freak out if I take it!"

She told me to go outside and get my dogs and wait for her in the car. I did as she said. I realize that it sounds like we cleaned Travis out and took everything, but I only took what my family had given us for wedding gifts, my personal belongings, Travis' old double bed, and the couch. I left him the television, stereo, armchair, and ottoman, the coffee table and matching end tables, the kitchen table and chairs, the dining room table and chairs along with the china cabinet, and the new bedroom suite that was my gift from him the previous Christmas. As I drove my car over to my dad's house, I kept glancing at the flatbed truck in the rearview mirror. One thought kept running over and over in my mind...Travis is going to kill me!

I had reason to feel this way because Travis had demonstrated his temper to me time and again in our relationship and I had never really crossed him before. I spent our entire relationship trying to please Travis, and I always did exactly what he told me to do. Taking the furniture was an enormous act of rebellion on my behalf, and I was afraid of the repercussions of my defiance. We stopped at a mini-storage warehouse and placed most of my belongings there. I was afraid to put my name on the paperwork, so we used the name of one of the girls from Mom's office. Her name was Paula, but we used her middle name, Gail, on the contract. I wouldn't have put it past Travis, once he'd found out what I'd done, to call every storage company between our house and my dad's to see if they had anyone listed as either "Karen Tritt" or "Karen Binette."

When I arrived at my father's house, he was outside waiting. Kevin had called him and apprised him of the situation. He was expecting us. We all went into the house to sit down and talk. Everyone left except for my brothers and two of their friends. Paula and her sister Pam were good friends of Kevin's. At the time, he was the lead singer and guitarist for a rock-and-roll band called "Double Exposure". Pam and Paula came to a lot of the rehearsals and all of the gigs that his band played. They had become constant fixtures at my dad's house, since Kevin still lived there. Dad told me that I needed to call Travis at work and tell him what I had taken out of the house. He said that Travis would be angrier if he walked into the house and saw that I had taken things without his knowing about it beforehand. I picked up the phone and dialed the number with shaking hands. My father stood right in front of me and held my hands for support. When Travis answered the phone I said, "It's me. I just wanted to let you know that I'm out of the house."

"What did you take?" he asked me coldly. "Oh, you know... my clothes, my hair dryer, the couch, my make-up... "

Travis interrupted me with a blood-curdling scream. I have never in all my life heard a grown man scream like that.

He shouted at me "You took WHAT? You had better get MY stuff back into MY house before I get home! I want my stuff back NOW!" I broke down sobbing and handed my father the phone. I had no intentions of returning the items that I had taken from my home. Travis would arrive home that evening, and I felt he might hurt me. My dad caught me because I was starting to fall to the ground under the weight of what had just happened. As my father held me in his arms, I looked over his shoulder and saw my twin brother Kevin crying silently in the kitchen. I had never seen him cry before, and that just added to my grief. He later told me that it nearly killed him to see me so upset. I told Dad what Travis had said. He looked at Mom and said, "We've got to get her out of here. He'll be coming over here with a gun."

Chapter Eighteen

I was numb with shock. The last few minutes had completely drained me of every desire to go on with my life. Fortunately for me, my parents were less affected by Travis' melodramatic threats. My father pushed me out the kitchen door while my mother grabbed my suitcase and hurriedly threw it into the trunk of Paula's Camaro. "Take her to your house," my father told Paula. "He doesn't know you and has no idea where you live. She'll be safe there for a few days." My mother kissed me and told me not to worry. She said that my father and my brothers would protect me and assured me that Travis would do me no harm as long as they were living. Pam, Paula's sister, got into the back seat and we drove away. They lived in Bartow County, Georgia which was about a forty-minute drive from my father's house. That left me plenty of time to mull over the events of the last few hours. In one day, I had gone from being on the verge of a peaceful trial separation with my husband to running for my life from the very same man. Even if Travis never made good on the threats to me and my family, just the fact that he had said those horrible words made me think that our relationship was almost past repair. How could a sane, rational man become so incensed over a sofa? The events had snowballed in the last two days and I had never felt more out of control of my life.

As we drove north, Pam and Paula said very little to me. I suppose that they didn't know what to say, since they didn't really know me that well. In retrospect, it was very kind and brave of them to put themselves in the middle of a dangerous domestic situation. Inside, I was spinning out of control, but somehow I felt that I had to appear calm. I was so emotionally drained that time seemed to be passing slowly... like the beating of my broken heart.

We eventually arrived at their home, and I was introduced to their family. Their mother was very sweet, and she took me in much as a mother hen takes in an abandoned chick. She hugged me and showed no worry, saying only that it would all work out somehow. Those were just the words that I needed to hear. She talked to me and comforted me for the entire five days that I stayed with them, hiding from Travis.

Someone told me that Travis was looking for me all over Marietta. He never did go to my house that day, though the men in my family were ready and waiting if he did show up. Kathie told me later that he went to her house and angrily demanded that she tell him where I was. He knew that we were friends and assumed that if anyone would know my whereabouts, it would be Kathie. She was telling him the truth when she said that she had no idea where I was.

I lived in fear for those five days. I was terrified of what Travis would do if he found me before he had had a chance to calm down. Pam's older brother suggested that I get a temporary restraining order against Travis. I thought that was a good idea. Travis would find out that I was so frightened of him, I had gone so far as to take legal steps to keep him away from me. Maybe that piece of information would convince him that this time he had gone too far.

I contacted a magistrate's office in Cobb County. They told me that I could not file a restraining order against my own husband without a divorce action pending. I spent hours that night trying to decide what to do. I didn't want to divorce Travis, even then. I just wanted him to calm down enough so that I could have a rational conversation with him. Calling him was absolutely out of the question. I knew that in my fragile emotional state I would not be able to stand up to another verbal assault. I was trying to protect our marriage by not filing for divorce, and I was trying to protect myself from bodily harm by obtaining the restraining order. In the end, my instinct for survival won out and I made a trip to an attorney's office.

My parents had recommended that I see the lawyer who had handled their divorce. He was a well-respected member of the legal community with a reputation of fairness. When I arrived and was ushered into his plush office, I broke down and began to weep. He was very compassionate and told me that divorce can be an emotionally painful experience. I explained to him through my tears that I didn't really want to divorce my husband. I just needed to file the papers in order to obtain the paperwork that would keep Travis a safe distance from me. He nodded his head as if to say "I know... I've heard all of this one too many times."

After signing the documents which would start the process of legally ending my marriage, I was too emotionally drained to walk across the street and file the paperwork for the restraining order. I wanted to go home. I could not stay and hide in Bartow County forever. I needed my family. I drove to Pam and Paula's house, packed my things, hugged them, thanked them profusely for their hospitality and generosity, and went home. My father was surprised to see me when I arrived. He expressed concern for my safety, and I reassured him by telling him that enough time had passed. In my opinion, if Travis was going to act out his anger he would have done so by now. I felt stronger that day than I had in a long time.

Filing for the divorce made me feel as if I had taken control over the events instead of the events controlling me. Much later that night, close to midnight, I finally worked up enough nerve to call my husband. He answered the phone calmly and remained so when I identified myself. The first thing he did was to ask me if I was all right. This question threw me off. The last thing I expected was for him to be concerned about me. I cautiously told him that I was okay. We talked for a few minutes, trying to gauge each other's position. He said he was still angry at me for taking the sofa. I explained to him that with the marriage becoming so rocky, I didn't know if he would want to reconcile after the separation. If not, I didn't want to walk away from a three-and-one-half-year relationship with nothing. If things did work out for us, he would have had the sofa again as soon as I moved back in. Travis didn't really understand my rationale and said as much. After a few more minutes, I decided that I needed to inform him that I had filed for a divorce, and tell him why.

Travis didn't like surprises, as I had so recently discovered. It wouldn't have been a great idea for him to learn of the divorce action via a county sheriff arriving at his front door, ready to serve him papers. His reaction was so unexpected, though it shouldn't have been in view of his past behavior. He began to yell again. "FINE! If that's what you want, then that's just FINE with me!"

I said "Honey, that's not what I want at all. I told you why I did it. I want us to work this out and be together. All that I have to do is call the lawyer and he'll stop the paperwork... "

"Oh, NO!" Travis interrupted. "A divorce is what you want and a divorce is what you'll get! I'll see you in court!" He slammed down the phone. I dissolved into tears as my last hope for saving my marriage disappeared before my eyes. I knew that there was no way I was going to convince him that a divorce was the last thing I wanted. Travis viewed my seeing an attorney as an act of aggression on my part. He wasn't about to let me get away with it. I would pay, and pay dearly, for my actions.

Chapter Nineteen

I received my copy of the divorce papers a few days later. I discovered that I was to spend my twenty-first birthday in divorce court. Our court date was set for June 11, 1984. Even after receiving the official documents, I still couldn't believe that this was actually happening.

I wondered to myself how things had managed to get so completely out of control. I also wondered how I had become the plaintiff in a divorce that I never even wanted.

Travis called me after he was served his copy of the paperwork. The initial document stated my wishes—actually, they were my attorney's. I was asking for all the items that I had taken, as well as alimony, and for Travis to pay my attorney's fees. My father had offered to pay the $500 for my lawyer on the condition that I take back my maiden name of Binette. I agreed, but felt that I needed to consider the money a loan. I wanted to repay him. In my opinion, he had helped pay for the wedding, even though he didn't particularly like my choice of a husband. It didn't seem fair to me that he had to pay even more money for me to divorce that same man.

Travis was not happy with my legal requests and suggested a private meeting so that we could perhaps come to an understanding. I agreed to meet him in the parking lot of our old high school on a

Saturday afternoon. Upon arriving, I climbed into the truck with him and we drove to the heating and air conditioning warehouse where he was still employed. I was very nervous about being alone with Travis in a deserted building, but love can affect your capacity for making logical decisions. Even then, I believed somewhere deep in the bottom of my heart that this was all a terrible nightmare, and that we would wake up the next morning and laugh about the silliness of the dream. I was innocent enough to believe that we could still be together.

We spoke very little on the drive. I could sense that this was not going to be a very productive meeting. Travis had a key to the office, and we quietly let ourselves in. We sat down across an old, scarred metal desk and began to talk, trying to come up with a solution that felt fair to both of us. Travis bluntly stated his proposal. "You give me back everything that you took, I won't pay you any alimony, you pay for your own attorney and I'll give you $600 in cash," he said. As I look back on it now, laughing was probably the worst thing that I could have done at that moment. I couldn't help it, though. His offer was ludicrous. He was suggesting that he keep everything and I, in essence, walk away with nothing. I flatly refused his offer. He became furious with me and told me that facing him in court would be the worst decision that I had ever made. He stated that he was aware of my phone conversations with Jimmy, and that he would make sure that everyone knew of my true character. He said that he would "drag my name through the mud in the newspapers," and that when he was through, no one would even consider going on a date with me.

I never did understand that statement. It was certainly not a crime to talk to another man on the phone while you were married to someone else, even if you did discuss marital problems and even possible solutions. Little did I know that Travis would eventually subpoena Jimmy into court and try to imply that he and I had had an adulterous affair. We argued for a few more minutes, then I told Travis that we obviously were not going to able to reach an agreement by ourselves and suggested that he take me back to my car. That was the last time that I saw him until we appeared in court together on my birthday.

My mother went with me for moral support. Even though she had been denied contact with me throughout the duration of my marriage, she was there for me during the agonizing experience of my divorce. When we walked into the courtroom, we saw Travis and his father James sitting on the left side of the room. Mom and I sat across from them on the right. I kept glancing at Travis, trying to determine his mood. He did not once speak to his father that I saw and just stoically stared ahead. There were several cases on the docket ahead of ours. "Tritt vs. Tritt" was number twelve or thirteen on the list that day. We were resigned to a long wait.

Even though it was a disastrous day for me emotionally, Mom and I were able to find the humor in an incident involving both Travis and his father. The first case to be called that day was a group of people who were suing a major corporation. The judge asked for all persons involved in that particular case to rise and remain standing until further instructed. We glanced to the left just in time to see both Travis and James stand up with about ten or twelve other people. It struck us as extremely funny. We only laughed harder when they looked at us to see if we were standing also, and hurriedly sat down when they realized that they had made a mistake.

My laughter stopped the instant that it became my turn to take the witness stand. Our case came up fairly rapidly, as there were problems with almost all of the cases before us that prevented them from being heard that day. Since I was the plaintiff, I took the stand first. A judge had to hear our case because Travis was contesting my legal petition. There would be no jury, and the judge would make all of the final decisions. My attorney pleaded my case and informed the judge that I had been emotionally battered. He portrayed me as a loving wife who wanted nothing more in this world than to please her domineering husband. He asked for the divorce on the grounds of irreconcilable differences.

I, surprisingly enough, did not break down and cry on the stand. The entire experience seemed unreal to me, as if I were watching a movie. In order to survive mentally that day, I distanced myself much as Scarlett O'Hara did on the day that Rhett Butler left, saying to myself "I won't think about this today... I'll think about it tomorrow when I can deal with it."

When I was through telling my side of the story, it was Travis' turn. He was sworn in and then began telling the judge that he couldn't live with me any more, saying that I was constantly wanting to be with him, I made unreasonable sexual demands of him, and I was too dependent on him for my emotional well-being. Travis' lawyer asked to call a witness to the stand. Travis stepped down and the attorney called Jimmy into the courtroom. After he took the stand, the attorney looked at Jimmy and said, "Can you identify the plaintiff?" He said yes and pointed to me. The lawyer said "Can you tell me her name?" Jimmy answered, "Karen Tritt." At that point, the judge interrupted and asked if Jimmy's testimony was going to be applicable in this case. When Travis' lawyer wouldn't give him a straight answer and only mumbled something about possible sexual misconduct on my part, the judge became frustrated and directly asked Jimmy "Have you ever kissed the plaintiff, Karen Tritt?" When Jimmy answered truthfully "No, Sir," the judge asked one final question. "Have you ever had sexual intercourse with Mrs. Tritt?" When Jimmy again truthfully answered no, the judge became irritated and said, "Get this man out of my courtroom. His testimony is not relevant."

Travis' lawyer's obvious attempt to sway the judge's feelings against me seemed to have had the opposite effect. He appeared to be leaning in my favor. In his closing arguments, my attorney stood up and stated, "Your Honor, in all my years as an attorney handling divorce cases, I have never once heard a husband make the statement in a court of law that his biggest problem was that his wife loved him too much," and then he sat down. That was it. No big speech about how I deserved the possessions that I had taken. No mention of the fact that because Travis had side jobs playing in the band, he made considerably more money than I did and therefore I deserved some financial help from him. I was a little dismayed about this until I heard the judge's ruling. Travis was to pay me $750 for my attorney's fee, $250 a month in alimony for a six-month period of time, and I was able to keep all of my belongings except the couch. Travis was awarded custody of his precious velour sofa. That was fine with me, since I didn't really like it in the first place. I had ten days to return the couch, and Travis was to begin making payments to me as of July 1, 1984.

Our day in court was the last time that I saw Travis that summer until we ran into each other at a wedding on August 25th. Travis and I had two mutual friends who had been dating for quite a while. Tim and Leigh decided to get married and asked Travis to sing. I did not know until I arrived at the church that my ex-husband had also received an invitation. When I walked in and heard him playing "Annie's Song", I almost turned around. I knew that there was no way that I was going to be able to sit through the wedding and watch Travis sing love songs without breaking down completely. I chose to stay, and surprised myself by making it through the ceremony with a minimum of tears.

When the wedding was over, I walked outside into the bright sunlight. As I was standing in the parking lot trying to compose myself, I looked up and saw Travis standing in front of me. "Are you okay?" he asked. I just nodded my head in reply. He took my arm and led me away from the crowd leaving the church. We walked over and sat down on a bench under a large oak tree. We spoke quietly for a few moments about trivial things. His next statement took me completely by surprise. He said that he had recently seen a psychic, who had acurately described the recent events of his life and also made a rather unbelievable prediction regarding his music.

Chapter Twenty

With my heart in my throat, I asked Travis what the psychic had said.

"She told me that I had recently been through a major break-up of some kind, either the ending of a long-term relationship or a divorce," he answered. "She also told me that the girl's name began with the letter 'C' or 'K'. I told her that the break-up was a divorce and that your name was Karen." Travis nearly caused me to stop breathing with his next revelation. The psychic had said to him "Do you know that she is trying to come back to you?" He asked me if this were true and I simply replied, "Yes, it's true." Travis put his arms around me and just held me for the longest time. All of the emotion that I had been holding back during the wedding ceremony that day began pouring out of me. Through my tears, I said to him, "I'm so sorry. I never meant for this to happen. I never wanted to hurt you. I'm so, so sorry Travis. Please forgive me." I told him that the previous two months had been the hardest of my life. Being without him was killing me, and I had no idea how I was going to survive. I thought of him every minute of every day. I had promised God that if He would only give Travis back to me, I would never ask for anything else as long as I lived. Travis seemed moved by my declaration, and assured me that we would talk about our situation.

He then told me some exciting news regarding his musical ambitions. The psychic had informed him that within a year, Travis would get an opportunity to go to Nashville. She strongly advised him to walk through this door when it opened for him. She said that it would change his life. She was absolutely correct. We left each other that day with a promise to talk again soon.

I left the church with my heart yet again filled with hope. If our love for each other was still strong enough for a psychic to be able to detect, then maybe we were meant to be together after all. I felt as though God was giving me one last chance to make things work. I wasn't about to disappoint Him. I planned to do everything in my power to win back my husband!

Travis called me a few days later, and during our conversation, informed me that he was playing a solo gig at a local lounge. Southern Bred had disbanded after Travis had Jimmy subpoenaed to testify at our divorce hearing. Travis was truly now a solo act—no wife, no band. Just him, his truck, his sofa, and his guitar.

I was sitting at my dad's house that Friday night when I made the decision to surprise Travis at the club. I dressed carefully, choosing an outfit that I knew he liked, and made the short trip to the bar. I walked in and stood in the entryway for a few moments to allow my eyes to adjust to the dim lighting. I heard Travis before I actually saw him. I closed my eyes and just listened for a while. Hearing his voice was soothing to my soul. I felt as though we had been apart for years instead of months. I made my way through the maze of tables to the back of the room. As luck would have it, there was an empty table directly in front, about four feet away from him. I sat down and stared right at him. His face registered surprise... then he smiled. All the hope in the world was in that smile.

He continued to sing until it came time for his break. He was sitting on a stool, playing soft romantic songs on his twelve-string guitar. The ambience of the lounge was that of a piano bar. The customers were mainly couples and the room was about half full.

When break time arrived, I felt the familiar sense of pride when Travis came directly to my table. We were talking quietly and holding hands when a girl walked up to the table and angrily asked him what he was doing. He told her to call someone else to come and get her since he would not be taking her to her home that night. She made an angry retort and stomped away to use the pay phone.

I was very embarrassed. It had never even occurred to me that Travis may have had a date. When I said this to him, he patted my hand and told me that she meant nothing to him and for me not to worry about it. I was ecstatic that he had chosen me over her! With each passing event, I became even more convinced that we would be reunited soon.

Travis had two or three more sets to play that night, and I gladly stayed until he was through. After we walked outside, he told me that he was going to go to one of his favorite hang-outs, a place near our high school called "Chico Dill's." He asked me if I would like to join him, and I readily accepted his invitation. On the way to the club, we were talking about our new living arrangements. I told him that my father didn't like having Sandy and Honey in the house as they were too big. Dad wanted to fence in the backyard, but our finances were a little tight. Travis offered to purchase the fence and install it himself. He would eventually spend an entire weekend fencing in my father's backyard for the dogs. I thought it was extremely sweet and thoughtful of him.

We finished our conversation just as we pulled up to the club. Travis had played before at Chico Dills and had acquired a small following. He was somewhat of a celebrity among the bar crowd there. When we walked in, several people greeted him by name and a large group of people asked us to sit with them. Travis introduced me to everyone by saying, "This is my ex-wife, Karen." You could have heard a pin drop in the small club. A woman turned to me and said, "So... you're the inspiration for all of those love songs that Travis has written!" I just laughed. We stayed at the bar for about an hour, then he walked me outside to my car. We were having an awkward moment. What does an ex-wife say to her ex-husband at a time like this? We were no longer married, but yet had been through so much together that we were not just friends either. We were somewhere in the middle, and we did what came naturally. Travis leaned down and kissed me very softly at first, but his kiss became more passionate and our emotions came to the surface. He finally released me and promised to call me soon.

My emotions intensified as I was driving home. The whole encounter that night was so bittersweet. I felt as though my heart were on a yo-yo string. The highs were so exhilarating, and the lows were so miserable. I wondered if I would survive long enough to see the end of this roller-coaster ride. I was feeling dejected in spite of the pleasant evening that I had just spent with Travis. It was almost more depressing to go home now that I felt some hope for rekindling our romance. I wanted to be with him, and I hated the fact that we were both going home to be alone when we should have never been apart to begin with. I felt my emotions overwhelming me and I knew that I needed someone to talk to.

By now, it was around three o'clock in the morning. I knew of only one person who would not only be awake at this time, but who would also provide me with a strong shoulder to cry on. My twin brother Kevin was a supervisor for a grocery store that was located near my father's house. He worked the night shift, and I knew that he was working that night. I quickly drove to the store and went inside. There were few customers there at that time of night. I walked over to the customer service counter and just stood there crying until Kevin happened to look down and notice me. He took one look at me and said, "Just stay right there. I'll see if I can go on break. Meet me in the deli."

When he came over a few minutes later, he sat down across the booth from me and said "Now, tell me what is wrong. Are you okay? Did something happen?" I shook my head and cried harder. When I finally could talk, I told him of my evening. I said that it was making me crazy to be apart from Travis. I didn't know how I was going to get him back, or even if I would remain sane long enough to do it. Kevin tried to comfort me by telling me that if it was meant to be, we would be together. If not, I would meet someone else because, after all, I was a "fox." He had never once, in the entire twenty-one years that we'd been siblings, made a positive comment to me regarding my appearance. It made me feel better to know that my own brother considered me to be attractive. I hugged him in thanks and went home.

I was in my room later that night, crying and talking to God. I told Him that I knew that He had said in the Bible that he would never give me a burden that I couldn't bear, but that maybe He had made a mistake this time. Maybe He had been taking a nap when the angels decided to hand me the events of the last three months. I told Him that my heart was literally breaking in two and that I really couldn't handle this by myself. I stopped crying the instant that I heard the words "My Child, you don't have to." An indescribable sense of peace came over me at that moment, and I knew somehow that I was going to be okay. I thanked God for listening to my prayers and fell asleep.

I awoke the next morning determined to return to my church. I had stopped going because, although Travis no longer attended, most of his family members did. It would have been too awkward to have to face his aunts and uncles and cousins every Sunday. I now felt as though I could handle it. I would really lean on God two days later.

Travis called me to tell me that he could no longer see me. His father had learned that he was seeing me again and had obviously expressed his disapproval. I suppose that Travis decided to listen to his father this time. I couldn't believe it when he broke the news. I had willingly cast my own mother aside for him during our marriage, and he wasn't willing to fight for me in the end. My spirit was broken, and after that conversation I no longer felt I had the strength to fight for our relationship. My hopes had been dashed once too often. I was done.

In May of 1985, I received the letter asking me to "keep the memories, but bury the love." The first part came easily. However, the second half would take me four years to accomplish.

Travis was invited to visit Nashville in the summer after we were divorced to become a full-time musician. I eventually moved in with my mother and tried to pick up the pieces of my shattered life. I had to find new owners for Sandy and Honey because Mom didn't have room for them. I felt as though I was losing everything that had ever been dear to me. I remember once when I came home from work and began to sob uncontrollably. Mom asked me what was wrong. I sat on the floor with my head in my hands and told her, "I'm so depressed! I'm NEVER, EVER going to love anyone as much as I love Travis!" She answered me with the wisdom that only a mother possesses and said, "Think about it, Karen... do you really want to?" I thought about that for a while and then came to a realization. Our Lord God was the only one who deserved to be worshipped. I was quite sure that I wouldn't love another man in the way that I had loved Travis, but maybe that wasn't such a bad thing after all. In my opinion, it is a horrible thing to love someone so much that you lose yourself along the way. I vowed that I would not make the same mistake twice. I've kept my promise.

Epilogue

My life has taken many twists and turns in the ten years since my divorce from Travis. I, like everyone else, have done good deeds and bad ones. One of the better achievements of my life happened when I introduced Paula to Travis' cousin, Daryl. I saw Daryl every Sunday in church and we remained good friends. It dawned on me one day that Paula and Daryl would be a perfect match. They were both soft spoken, gentle Christian souls. They had similar backgrounds and personalities. I coaxed Paula into accompanying me one Sunday morning. The sparks flew the minute that they met. They were married six months later, and are approaching their eleventh wedding anniversary. They have a beautiful young son named Cody. Paula continues her work as an x-ray technologist at the same doctor's office that Mom used to manage. I talk to her from time to time just to see how they are doing. It is ironic to me that Paula first became aware of Travis through me, and because of my actions she is now his cousin-in-law! I made a life for myself as a single woman. I knew that I had been scarred too deeply to even think about marriage for a long time.

I still thought about Travis and wondered how he was. In the fall of 1985, I learned that he had remarried. I have no idea what their marriage was like. I've often wondered if Travis treated her the same way that he treated me. I do not know the details of their divorce in

1989, only that I was told it was a mutual decision. I stayed away from Travis for three years. Even though he was distanced from me physically, I still held him close in my heart. I had an opportunity to confront Travis in the spring of 1988.

My brother Kevin had married Becky a year and a half earlier, and Becky had heard all of the family stories about Travis but had never seen him in person. Mom, Becky, and I had gone out to dinner one night. On our way home we passed a Krispy Kreme doughnut shop, and Becky developed a sudden urge for doughnuts. She was six months pregnant with my niece, Lindsey. After going through the drive-through window and picking up a dozen raised honey-dips for Becky, we started on our way home. We passed a small brick lounge on Roswell Road, in Marietta. A sign out front stated that Travis Tritt was to be the evening's entertainment. Becky yelled at Mom to pull in there, and we drove into the uncrowded parking lot. Becky slowly got out of the car and walked up to the large plate glass window in front of the building. She tried to stand on her tiptoes to see into the window, but this was extremely difficult as she was very pregnant! Becky finally opened the front door and stuck her head inside. The stage was right inside the door, and Travis was only about twelve feet away. I jumped behind the wall, my heart pounding. What if he had seen me? What was I going to say? I begged Becky to close the door while my mother started laughing. We were acting very immature and Mom said, "Oh, you guys... this is so HIGH SCHOOL!"

A waiter from inside the bar opened the door and asked us if he could be of service. Becky, not one to be shy, spoke up and said "No, thank you. This is Travis Tritt's ex-wife and I'm her sister-in-law. I've never seen him, so we just stopped by for a minute." If I didn't love her so much, I would have punched her! "Oh, great!" I said. "Now that waiter is going to tell Travis that his ex-wife was standing outside and that she was too afraid to go inside!" We continued to laugh about that incident all the way home. It is still a big joke in our family today.

It was after this that I changed careers once again. I was bored working at the salon. My salary wasn't really enough to help me make ends meet. I accepted a manager's position at a local singing telegram company. The pay was excellent and I absolutely loved this job! It was a very stylish company. We did tasteful, funny routines for birthdays, anniversaries, almost any occasion that you can think of. We didn't have strippers or anything along that line, just good clean fun. I stayed at this job for three wonderful years.

This was where I was working when I received a phone call from my old friend Kathie in the spring of 1989. We had not seen each other in five years. I can't remember how she located me, but I was very happy to hear from her. We arranged to meet for dinner in a popular restaurant outside Atlanta. She was there waiting when I arrived. Kathie looked great! She was always very beautiful, and she had grown and matured in the years since I had seen her. She looked sleek and sophisticated. She was working as an executive for a large corporation. She and Mark, Southern Bred's old banjo player, had divorced some time ago. Kathie said she had a surprise for me. I turned around and our old friend Michelle was walking through the door. I couldn't believe my eyes! Michelle had grown up to be a stunning young woman. She was tall, with long gorgeous blonde hair and a terrific figure. I couldn't believe that this beautiful, self-assured woman had been a gawky, quiet teenager only a few years ago.

After we were seated at our table, Michelle told me that she was employed as a dancer at one of Atlanta's top adult entertainment clubs. We talked and laughed and generally caught up on each other's lives for several hours. They asked me if I had been in contact with Travis. When I told them no, they said, "Then you haven't heard the news." "What news?" I asked, puzzled. "He's getting a divorce," they replied. A funny feeling started in the bottom of my stomach. The fire had died in my heart the day that I found out about his second marriage. With this new revelation, the flame began to flicker just a bit. "A divorce," I said to myself. This warranted further investigation. They also let it slip that Travis was currently playing at a large, popular country bar and dance club called "Miss Kitty's."

It was 1989, and country music was making a huge comeback. Country bars were springing up all over Atlanta. Miss Kitty's was considered to be the best. It was at this location that Travis would eventually film his first music video, "Country Club."

After parting with Kathie and Michelle amid hugs and promises to keep in touch, I drove to the apartment that I shared with two other girls. I thought of nothing but Travis for the next few days.

I eventually decided that I was going to have to go and see him if I was going to have any peace. It took me forever to choose my outfit for my first meeting with my ex-husband in five years. I finally decided on a pastel blue and yellow flowing skirt with a white, off-the-shoulder, lace-trimmed peasant blouse. I gathered my long hair into a loose pony tail and placed a wide-brimmed straw hat on my head. I wore very little make-up. I looked sexy, feminine and natural... just the way he liked.

I convinced my roommate Kimber to accompany me to the bar. Even though she disliked country music, she was curious about my former husband. It was a Friday night and the place was packed. We found an empty table upstairs, near a balcony overlooking the stage. It was perfect! I could see Travis clearly, but he couldn't see me. As he began to play, all the old familiar feelings that I had tried so hard to bury began to well up in my heart. He looked so handsome standing on stage, surrounded by his new band. He wasn't as flamboyant a performer as he is today, though he was still compelling to watch. I sat mesmerized until it was time for them to take a break. Travis began talking to some fans who were seated just in front of the stage. I gathered my nerve and went downstairs to see him. He was about six feet away, with his back to me. My hands were sweaty and I was sure that he could hear my heart thumping. I had no idea what I was going to say or how I was going to be received. He must have felt me staring at him, because he slowly turned around and looked right into my eyes. I stopped breathing. He walked toward me, held out his arms as if to hug me, and then stopped short. I smiled and said, "It's okay... I won't bite you." He smiled in return and wrapped his arms around me and gave me a big hug. He seemed delighted to see me and my heart soared! "How are you?" he asked. I told him that I was wonderful and returned the question to him. "Well," he replied. "I'm getting a divorce." "I know... I heard. I'm very sorry," I said. He shrugged his shoulders and then lightened the mood by saying, "Oh well. I must be difficult to live with or something!" Understatement of the year.

He asked me where I was sitting and told me that he would join me at my table shortly. I rejoined Kimber and patiently waited until he arrived. We sat and talked for the entire break. When I told him of my job at the singing telegram company, he grinned and said, "That is a perfect job for you. You always did have a great voice." The compliment made me feel very good. Travis went on to tell me that our divorce was not a total loss for him. He said, "I have gotten at least twenty good songs out of our break-up." When it was time for him to return to the stage, he hugged me again and handed me an autographed copy of his first album. I have since misplaced the album, but I do remember the words that were inscribed on the front cover. "To Karen, my first wife: Thank you for your love all those years. Maybe I'll see you again in another five years! Love, Travis."

Clutching my record, I stood to leave until I heard him say over the microphone, "This next song is for my ex-wife, Karen." I abruptly sat down. The song was entitled "I'm Not Laughing Now." It told of our great love for each other, how we met in high school, our marriage, and our subsequent divorce. The hook line for the song is "I've heard it said, 'Ain't love funny', but I'm not laughing now." Travis stared at the area of the balcony where he knew that I was sitting. He wasn't just singing this song about me, he was singing it to me. I couldn't handle it. When the song was over, I jumped up and ran outside to my car. My emotions were in such a tangle. How could he still affect me this way after all these years? Watching him on the stage that night, I saw the Travis that I had fallen in love with. I didn't see the man who hurt and humiliated me. I didn't see the man who taken me on a two-year emotional roller-coaster ride. I didn't see the man who threatened my life when I crossed him. I only saw the good. Seeing him again made me remember why I had loved him so in the first place.

That last song had stirred a whole host of emotions that I had thought to be long dead. I managed to hold myself together until about one o'clock the next afternoon. I was sitting in my office at work when the tears came without warning. I asked one of the girls to cover for me and I went outside and sat down on the grass under a large tree. I sobbed for five straight hours. I tried to stop when my best friend Burge came outside. She put her arms around me and told me to let it all out. Obviously, I had repressed a lot of the emotion surrounding my divorce. Seeing Travis again had opened the floodgate. Even though I was completely drained after my ordeal, I somehow felt better, as if a great weight had been lifted from my heart.

Burge decided to sell the singing telegram company in the summer of 1989, and I knew I didn't want to work there without her. Burge and I were not just employer and employee, we were soul friends. She had helped me through many a crisis in my life. We had another best friend named Donna Summers, who is one of the foremost talent agents for film and television in Atlanta. She always stays extremely busy and she needed another agent to help with her heavy workload. I gratefully accepted the position. I made the decision to get my own studio apartment in an eclectic section of Atlanta known as Virginia Highlands. I needed some extra money to furnish the apartment, so I began moonlighting at the new "Miss Kitty's" in downtown Atlanta. After working there for two months, I learned that Travis would be making a concert appearance on what would have been our seventh wedding anniversary, September 25, 1989. I was excited and nervous about seeing him again. I ran into

Travis in the office behind the stage. We spoke for a few minutes. He hugged me and I wished him well. It was sad to see him go, and yet I knew that I did not and could not fit into the life that he was making for himself. I felt that things were for the best. Travis was going on with his life, and I was going on with mine. Most of the time, I am able to forget that I was ever married to a country music star until someone asks me, "Did you *really* used to be married to Travis Tritt?" To which I reply, "No, Travis Tritt used to be married to me."

THE END